I0439536

**Jean-Paul Cassone'**

# BRICS and Mortar

**"The Polarity of geopolitics**

**from Tehran to Menlo Park"**

Printed in U.S.A. for CSRV

(Cassone' Silk Road Ventures)

*(Master proof printed at CreateSpace, a DBA of On-Demand Publishing LLC)

*(Cover art by graphic artist Bonnie B. Brewer, Compass Printing, Saranac Lake, N.Y.)

# About the Author

Towards the end of the 1990's to 2000 Jean-Paul Cassone' first began to surface strictly as a freelance international, geopolitical columnist for various newspapers in the Middle East and in China. During 2001 he relocated to Guangzhou, China in Guangdong Province where he lived for three years. At the time Mr. Cassone's real passion was to write English textbooks for Chinese lawyers. On the cusp of his first big break in that field "The 9-11 Incident" occurred and all 30 + lawyers who had enrolled in a very upscale and expensive educational package, for which he was chosen to be its sole editor and textbook writer, suddenly became spooked and abruptly withdrew from the program in unison. This was due to the package's itinerary which included flying to Seattle, Washington to meet with its mayor. The incident succeeded in frightening all of Cassone's potential clients away from the idea of flying into the U.S. .

Jean-Paul Cassone' then proceeded to feverishly teach English as a freelance independent where he taught scholastic, business, medical, legal, corporate and IELTS English to more than 4,000 students for over 25 separate schools ,universities, corporations and private entities such as: Nanhua University of Industry &

Commerce, China Army Medical Hospital, New Oriental School, Guangdong University for Foreign Studies minor school, Alcanta, China Com, English First, 2 Law Firms, Rockwell Automation, Whirlpool, Total-Fina-Elf, 3 levels of Kindergarten, Grades 1-5, all Middle School grades, all High School grades and 1st through 3rd years of College, China Army Physicians, Nurses, China Bank employee's , as well as China teachers, other professionals and casual adults! His disposition is fervent to always remaining young at heart and one might say that he possesses a very restless, yet positive soul with a zest to always remain in motion.

Following his return to the United States in 2004 he predominantly worked in the printing industry with a passion for alternative news. After having several news blogs online, "The Herald Traveller" once being the most popular of the bunch, he has recently become captivated by what he's coined as "the most unique time in all of American history" which he says will be coming to a most important and final fork in the road, sometime between 2016-2018.

Jean-Paul Cassone' is an outspoken "multipolarist" who warns us all that the 'Zionist-Israeli handlers' who took America hostage in 1963 are now taking the world to Armageddon based purely on gross orchestration and delusional assumptions. He recently stated, "Americans, Europeans and Russians were all perfectly set and ready to become much closer friends, both socially and in business. Then suddenly these inbred pack of elite, homicidal psychopaths who've hijacked 'the real United States' are proceeding to insist on not 'dismantling NATO', but rather to hoodwink us all into a 'back-to-the-future' shell game where we're all suddenly supposed to hate one another and reignite 'Cold War 2.0'. It's a complete and total archaic sham, completely instigated only for the purpose of lining the pockets of an Industrial Military Complex's privileged few"!

“When the devil is cornered he will commit suicide, but not until he’s certain he can take you with him”.

Jean-Paul Cassone’

(JPC-book 3)

# Table of Contents

# Chapter I

## A Supreme Leader

Ayatollah Sayyid Ali Hosseini Khamenei is the Supreme Leader of Iran. In the Islamic Republic of Iran he is the Supreme Leadership Authority, the Head of State and highest ranking political and religious Authority in the Islamic Republic of Iran. In accordance with the concept of Guardianship of the Islamic Jurists, the post was established by the constitution. Though the terminology found in the constitution of Iran refers to him as the "Leader", the title "Supreme Leader" is often used as a sign of respect.

Appointing the heads of many powerful posts in military, the civil government and the judiciary, the Supreme Leader is more powerful than the President of Iran. The constitution was amended in 1989 which permitted a leader to be a lower ranking cleric of Islamic "scholarship". Before this, it was required that the leader must be a "Marja'-e taqlid" in Usuli Twelver Shia Islam, the highest ranking cleric and authority in its religious laws. The Islamic Republic has had two Supreme Leaders in its history. From 1979-1989 Ruhoilah Khomeini held the position and holding the position since Khomeini's death it has been Ali Kamenei.

The Assembly of Experts elects the Supreme Leader. All candidates to the Assembly of Experts, the president and the Majlis are selected by the Guardian Council, whose members are selected by the Supreme Leader of Iran. Together with a two-thirds majority of the Parliament, any declaration of war or peace is to be made by the Supreme Leader.

In late November of 2015, Ayatollah Khamenei issued his second letter to the youth in Western countries. He described the bitter Terrorist events in France as a ground for deliberation. The

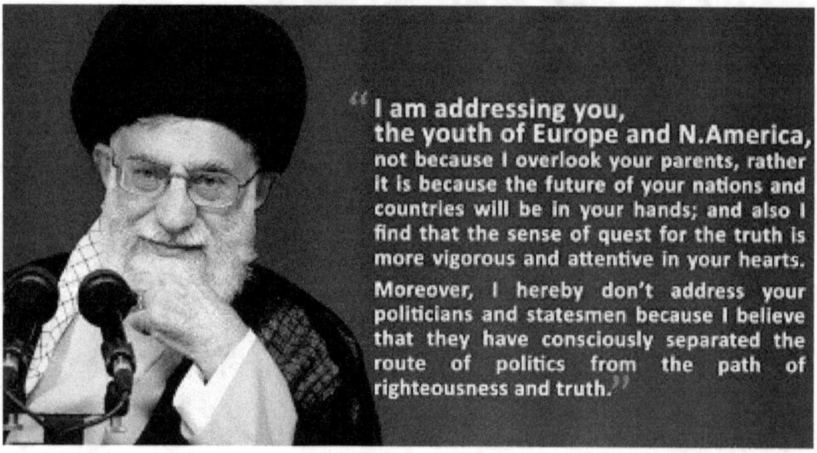
"I am addressing you,
the youth of Europe and N.America,
not because I overlook your parents, rather it is because the future of your nations and countries will be in your hands; and also I find that the sense of quest for the truth is more vigorous and attentive in your hearts.
Moreover, I hereby don't address your politicians and statesmen because I believe that they have consciously separated the route of politics from the path of righteousness and truth."

text of this historic letter of the Supreme Leader of the Islamic Revolution is as follows:

"In the Name of Allah, the Most Compassionate, the Most Merciful".

"To all the youth in Western countries",

"The bitter incidents triggered by blind terrorism in France, motivated me to once more talk to you, young people. In my view, it is regrettable that such events provide the ground for dialogue, but the reality is that if such painful issues do not provide the ground for finding a solution and a venue for consultation, the ensuing damage would be double".

"The suffering of every human being the world is per say, sorrowful for his fellow human beings. The scene of a child dying before the eyes of his beloved ones, a mother who's family's happiness turns into mourning, a husband carrying the lifeless body of his wife to somewhere hastily, or a spectator who is not aware that he is going to see the last sequence of his life in moments, are not scenes which would not stir sentiments and feelings".

"Anybody endowed with affection and humanity is affected and touched by the scenes, whether they occur in France, in Palestine, in Iraq, in Lebanon, or in Syria. Definitely one and a half billion Muslims share this feeling and abhor and loathe the perpetrators of these tragedies. But the important question is that if today's suffering do not end in building a better and safer future, they will be reduced to more bitter and fruitless memories. I believe that this is only you, the youth, who by learning lessons from today's hardships, will be able to find new solutions for building the future and block-off roads which have led the West to this current position".

"It is true that today terrorism is the pain we and you share, but it is necessary for youth to know that the insecurity and anxiety that you felt in the recent incidents, differ on two major grounds with the pain that people in Iraq, Yemen, Syria and Afghanistan have endured, throughout successive years. First of all, the Muslim world has been victim to terrorism and violence more extensively, on a much larger scale and for a much longer period of time. And the second difference is that unfortunately, these acts of violence have always been supported by big powers in different ways, in an effective manner".

"Today, barely is someone aware of the United States of America's role in the creation, or strengthening and arming of al-Qaeda, Taliban and other ominous followers. Alongside this direct support the palpable and known supporters of Takfiri terrorism, despite having the most primitive political establishments, have always been among the allies of the West and that is while the most progressive and the clearest thoughts born out of dynamic democracies in the region have been ruthlessly suppressed. The West's double standards vis-a'-vis the moment of awakening in the Muslim world is a telling example of contradiction in the Western policies".

"Another aspect of this contradiction, is seen in the West's support for Israel's State terrorism. The oppressed people of Palestine have been experiencing the worst kind of terrorism for more than 60 years. If the people in Europe have been taking refuge in their homes and been avoiding the gatherings and crowded centers, only for a number of days, it has been for tens of years that a Palestinian family has not been safe from the Zionist regime's carnage and destruction machines, even at its own home. What kind of violence could be compared today with the Zionist regime's settlement construction, in terms of its intense brutality"?

"Without having ever been seriously and effectively blamed by its influential allies, or at least the self-declared independent, international institutions, this regime has been demolishing the homes of Palestinians. Destroying their orchards and farmlands on a daily basis, without even giving them time to move their living properties, or collect their crops. All this is often taking place before the terrified and tearful eyes of women and children who witness the beating and injury of their family members and, in some cases, their transfer to notorious torture chambers. Do you know any other act of brutality on the same scale and dimension and at this rate of persistence in today's world? If shooting at a woman in the middle of the street, only for having protested a soldier armed to the teeth is not terrorism, so what is it? Should this barbarism not be labeled extremism just because it is being committed by the military forces of an occupying government? Or maybe these images should no longer stir our conscious, only because they have been constantly seen on T.V. screens for 60 years"?

"Military campaigns targeting the Muslim world over recent years, which have taken countless lives, are another example of the West's contradictory logic. Besides human losses, the invaded countries have lost their economic and industrial infrastructure, their drive towards growth and development has been halted, or slowed down and in some cases, turned back ten years. Nonetheless, they are rudely asked not to consider themselves oppressed. How can a country be reduced to ruins and its city and villages be reduced to ashes and then its people told not to consider themselves as oppressed? Instead of inviting people not to understand or forget about tragedies, isn't honest apology better? The pain endured by the Muslims world, due to the hypocrisy and insincerity of the aggressors is no less than material damage".

"Unfortunately these roots have also penetrated deeply into the cultural policies of the West through consecutive years and have led to a soft and silent onslaught. Many countries in the world take pride in their indigenous and natural culture; cultures that fed human communities for hundreds of years, at the same time they have been flourishing and reproducing. The Muslim world has been no exception to this rule. But in the contemporary period the Western world, benefitting from advanced tools, has been insisting on cultural simulation and unification in the world".

"I consider the imposition of the Western culture on other nations and the belittling of independent cultures as a silent and very harmful act of violence. Humiliating rich cultures and insulting their most respected parts are happening, while the alternative culture is by no means qualified enough to supplement them. For instance, the two elements of "aggressiveness" and "moral promiscuity" which have unfortunately turned into the main components of the Western culture, have downgraded in acceptability and standing, even in its own birthplace. The question now is, if we would be committing a sin if we rejected a belligerent, obscene culture that shuns spirituality? If we block the flood of destruction which is streaming towards our youth, in the form of quasi-artistic products, will we be guilty? I do not deny the significance and values of cultural bonds. These bonds have led to growth and prosperity and richness every time they have been made under natural conditions and through respect for the accepting society. On the contrary, incongruous and imposed bonds have proven to be unsuccessful and damaging".

"I regret to say that vile groups like Daesk are born out of unsuccessful bonding with imported cultures. If the problem was really ideological, such phenomena must have been seen in the Muslim world, before the era of colonialism as well. However, history proves the contrary. Historical evidence makes it clear how the colonial concurrence, with an extremist and ostracized mentality in the heart of a primitive tribe, planted the seed of radicalism in this region. Otherwise, how is it possible that a refuse like Daesh could have been burned out of one of the most ethical and the most humane religious ideologies in the world that, in its essential fabric, draws a parallel between killing a human being and killing the entire humanity"?

On the other hand, one must ask why some people who have been in Europe and grown up intellectually and spiritually in the same environment, are being attracted to this kind of group? Definitely one should not ignore the impact of a lifetime, unhealthy cultural feeding in a contaminated and violence-breeding environment. A comprehensive analysis must be carried out in this regard, an analysis to explore the overt and the covert sources of contamination of a society. Maybe the deep seated hatred that has been sown in the hearts of some social classes in the Western societies, throughout the years of industrial and economic prosperity was due to inequality at times, as a result of legal, structural discriminations and has given rise to the complexes that emerge from time to time in such a sickening manner".

At any rate, it is you who should break through the layers of your society, find knots and grudges and do away with them. Instead of being widened the rifts must be narrowed. The big mistake in fighting terrorism is hasty reactions that increase existing chasms. Any emotional and hasty move that would scare away and unsettle the Muslim community living in Europe and America, which compromises millions of active or responsible human beings and deprive them of their basic rights more than before and ostracizes them socially, will not only fail to solve any problems, but also increase distances and deepen grudges. Superficial and reactionary measures, particularly when legalized, will have no other outcome, but to clear the way for future crisis by increasing existing polarizations. According to reports received in some European countries, certain regulations have been adopted to obligate citizens to spy on Muslims. These behaviors are unjust and we all know that injustice produces reciprocal response".

"Furthermore, Muslims do not deserve such ingratitude. The Western world has known Muslims for centuries. The day that the Western people settled into the territory of Islam as guests they cast a covetous look on the wealth of their host. The day that they were the host and benefitted from the Muslim's work and thought, they mainly saw nothing in Muslims but kindness and patience.

Therefore I ask you the youth to lay the foundation for a proper and honorable interaction with the Muslim world, based on correct knowledge and deep insight and from learning lessons from past tragic experiences. In this case, in a not distant future you will see that the edifice you have erected on such a foundation, will spread the confidence and trust over the heads of its architects. Grant them the warm of security and calm and radiant rays of hope in a bright future on the world". (End of speech)

As any impartial viewer of the Middle East can see, "hypocrisy" and "double Standards" are predominantly found throughout Israeli and Western policies. Israel refused the late President Kennedy's request for "nuclear inspections" and then proceeded to act as an instrumental component to his assassination. "With no objections from the United States", Israel then and continuously has refused to sign any nuclear non-proliferation agreements, while it has been proven that Israel provided both supplies and strategic air transportation to the "Western created" ISIS terrorist group".

If Muslims are to be spied upon in Western society, "Whose watching the Zionists"? In this contemptuous light, I can only find hope in the Supreme Leader's September, 2015 statements, at the Imam Khomeini Mosque, as follows:

"I say to Israel that they will not see the end of these 25 years", as it relates to a recent nuclear agreement between Iran and the so-called P5 + 1, the United States, U.K., France, Germany, China and Russia. Since the agreement is pegged to a 25 year duration in certain regards, hence the Supreme Leader's reference to such a period and beyond continued, "God willing, there will be no such thing as a Zionist regime in 25 years. Until then, struggling, heroic and jihadi moral, will leave no moment of serenity for Zionists. We agree to hold talks with the Americans, only on the nuclear issue and for particular reasons and thank God, our negotiations did a good job".

The Supreme Leader's predecessor, the late Ayatollah Ruhollah Khomeini, often accused the United States of being "The Great Satan", whose truth in that statement is becoming increasingly clearer and clearer in the U.S. destruction of the Libyan democratic nation, as well as the grotesque actions in 9-11, Iran, Afghanistan and Syria. The accusation finds even further validity by the open use of U.S. soldiers to guard the world's heroine poppy supply in Afghanistan. Is it any wonder that "suicide" is the U.S. military's #1 cause of death today? The late Ayatollah Khomeini had further stated, "Some people insist on disguising this Great Satan as the 'Savior Angel'. However, the Iranian nation expelled this Satan from the country; we must not allow that when we expelled it through the door, it could not return and gain influence again, through the window".

Getting back to Iran's current Supreme Leader, Ayatollah Khamenei (just slightly different spelling), this past September, 2015 also found him addressing commanders of the elite Revolutionary Guards, as he warned them to be on the alert for "political and cultural" infiltration by the United States. Khamenei told a gathering of the guard commanders and personnel in Tehran, "The main purpose of the enemies is for Iranians to give up on their revolutionary mentality. Enemy means global arrogance, the ultimate symbol of which is the United States. Economic and security breaches are definitely dangerous and have dire consequences. But political and cultural intrusion by the enemy is a more serious danger that everyone should be vigilant about. The enemies are waiting for a time when the nation and system fall asleep, for example, in 10 years when I may not be here to realize their objectives. But the nation and the authorities won't let that happen".

After studying Iran's Supreme Leader, Ayatollah Sayyid Ali Hosseini Khamenei, it becomes evident that he is not only a profound spiritual leader, but like all leaders, such as Vladimir Putin who truthfully cares about his people, he demonstrates great wisdom in the careful balance between maintaining a nation's focus, while having that focus continue in such a harmony that is directly in-keeping with the times.

On November 23, 2015, Russian President Vladimir Putin gave the Iranian Supreme Leader one of the few copies of the original edition of the Muslim holy book, the Koran dating back some 1,500 years. The Prophet Muhammad died in 632 A.D. and Muslims believe that his teachings were God's instructions given to him directly. These teachings were memorized by his followers and orally passed on. Later on Osman in 651 A.D., the Muslim caliph or leader, decided to codify Muhammad's teachings in a single book. Of all Korans, only 5 Osman ones were ever created.

Following Osman's murder Ali his successor, brought the Osman Koran to northern Iraq, which the central Asian ruler Tamerlane conquered and pillaged during the 14$^{th}$ – 15$^{th}$ centuries. Samar Kand today's central Uzbekistan, was the capital of Tamerlane's vast empire where he ordered the Osman Koran to be stored. For four centuries Tamerlane's Osman Koran was stored in Samar Kand's majestic Khoja Ahrar Mosque. Later, during the

1800's and then known as Turkestan, Imperial Russia's conquering armies occupied Central Asia. The Russian Governor in 1869, had this same Koran sent to the Royal Library for storage in St. Petersburg. Fifty copies were ordered made, by ethnographers in 1905. Kept in libraries in St. Petersburg, only a handful of the copies which were printed 110 years ago remain.

Today Iran's future has never looked brighter, spiritually, culturally, economically, strategically and technologically it is proving to come into an ever fuller blossom as one of the Middle East's most shining examples of a humane and most prosperous trading nation. Just as Iran's Supreme Leader, its people are forever diligent, industrious, focused, patient and persevering, being always gracious to their God's and their Leader's Deliverance with a degree of appreciation that takes nothing for granted. It is from these evident truths that Iran shall prove to be a shining jewel in the crown of the BRICS multipolar head, as it ascends onto the world's center stage.

# Chapter II

## An Iron Rose

The 36th President of Brazil, Dilma Vana Rousseff was born in December of 1947 and is the country's first woman president. Raised in an upper middle class family in Belo Horizonte. Her father was a Bulgarian entrepreneur. During the 1960's she fought against the military dictatorship and was captured. It is reported that during this time 197-1972, she was also tortured.

She rebuilt her life after her release, in Porto Alegre with Carlos Araujo, a partnership that would later span some thirty years. In Rio Grande do Sol they helped found the Democratic Labor Party (PDT). In Porto Alegre she became the Secretary of the Treasury under Alceu Collares and later in Rio Grande do Sul, the Secretary of Energy for both Collares and Olivio Dutra. (*Reader's note: What makes compiling these facts accurately in as updated a version as possible, is proving to be a daunting task. At this writing, late-breaking news is currently reporting that Western shenanigans have successfully infiltrated her administration as I write this, in a slow motion coup attempt to impeach this great woman. In typical Washingtonian fashion, illegal bribes, threats and coercion are the suspected methods of choice likely being utilized.)

She then later left the PDT and joined the Worker's Party (PT). In a corruption scandal which later led to then Chief of Staff, Jose' Dirceu's resignation, Ms. Rousseff took over the post and later stepped down to run for president in March, 2010. You the reader should hereby be made aware of some very unique peculiarities about Brazil and the Brazilian culture. Latin America has always been a hotbed for Western Cold War espionage. The CIA has a notorious reputation here, along with its cousins at the World Bank and the IMF. What ratchets things up a notch is Brazilians have a proven "trust deficit". According to a 2014 survey by the National Confederation of Industry, 62% of Brazilians have little or no trust in most people anywhere.

As this book is being printed a new US-Brazilian Cold War has been put into motion. This can best be explained by one of the world's foremost global news networks, Russia's "Sputnik News" as follows:

"The reasons Washington wants to get rid of Dilma Rousseff, are easy to understand", Sputnik wrote. "She signed the agreement about the establishment of the (BRICS) New Development Bank". (This of course eliminates any further need to deal with either the World Bank or the IMF in the future. America's current Crime Cabal–type government is highly jealous of the following :) - "the construction of a 5,600 kilometer-long (about 3,200 miles) fiberoptic telecommunications system across the Atlantic to Europe, initiated by Ms. Rousseff herself. The new communications system would guarantee protection against foreign espionage and would undermine the U.S.-backed communications 'monopolies'. Telebras president told the local media that the project would be developed and implemented without the participation of any U.S. company".

"Rousseff has angered Washington by blocking the return to Brazil of major U.S. oil and mining companies, looking to China for investment instead". As this book is in production there is a covert, Western-backed operation "in-play" and full-swing through conspiracy, intimidating propaganda and corrupt and illegal means, to have Ms. Rousseff impeached. This makes it no small wonder then that in a deeper analysis of a 4 year Interpersonal Trust Index study, Brazil placed $54^{th}$ of $59^{th}$ among participating nations, in terms of the degree in which people trusted others around them. Unfortunately, the CIA is experienced in how to brainwash Brazilians who have a reputation for short memories. This makes them ideal candidates for political overthrow, regardless of if it were Saint Peter himself who was the sitting president.

These unfolding events all now make Ms. Rousseff's predicament one of the world's most glaring examples of the current United States' repugnant arrogance, blatant disregard for international law and a dangerously combustible loose-cannon-of-a –nation, which has become severely reckless and diabolical. It resonates to the entire free world in crystal clarity that the West has fully redeemed its glory days of being many things to be emulated, for a complete turnover into being all of the things it once flatly stood against. It is glaring evidence that the West's dying New World Order contraption has all along been led by the means of Zionist elitists like the Rothschilds, Rockefellers, George Soros and others, using the "former United States" as their tool, one-in-the-same-way as Israel and the new U.S. Industrial Military Complex used ISIS.

Due to President Rousseff's brusque manner and short temper she has been nicknamed "The Iron Lady". Her social reforms have lifted millions out of poverty and she has prided herself on investigating corruption claims, having sacked several ministers over corruption allegations. (*Reader's note: It is worthy of mention that the U.S. has often been associated with those making attempts to undermine her standing by means of misleading propaganda in a conduit to achieve a slow, eroding coup through falsely hyped corruption, hearsay and lies, in their destabilization practices. For example, a covert Western campaign was launched to discredit her very successful Olympic sponsorship achievements, by stirring up grass roots activists with the notions of it being portrayed as a foolish waste of taxpayer's revenues. The obvious booby prize in all of this being the State-run oil company Petrobas. Ms. Rousseff has also served on the Petrobas Board of Directors from 2003-2010).

Let's just stop the presses here a minute and reflect on what makes me write books like this for a second. The "new" United States, now as an Israeli colony is using U.S. taxpayers' money to "illegally overthrow covertly", a "democratically-elected government" for the sole benefit of "monopolizing conglomerates" of North America and already "super-wealthy Zionist globalist", "war-investment bankers", "weapons dealers" and "oil oligarchs"! In just this one Brazilian incident it instantly verifies the words of the late Ayatollah Khomeini's deducting wisdom. America now is "The Great Satan".

President Rousseff's "Bolsa Familia" has benefitted some 36 million Brazilians as a social welfare program and she recently announced a 10% increase in their payments. It is said that as a little girl she often aspired to dreams of becoming a ballerina. During her rigid captivity as a soldier she was referred to as the "high priestess of subversion". Having survived that tragedy, she was forced to rise to a second great challenge when she was diagnosed with lymphatic cancer in 2009.

But nothing could ever stand in her way. To win public support she underwent a complete makeover in 2010, including plastic surgery and teeth-whitening. This dazzling presidential fighter has been responsible for creating 5.4 million new jobs, fixing Brazil's new minimum wage at 724 reals, the highest since 1979, while reducing unemployment by 30% from 2008-2012. Brazil's economy is now one of the world's largest and exports have quadrupled. Based on low inflation and an increase in investment, is Brazil's sustainable development. Brazil hosted the Sixth New Development Bank summit in July of 2014 with BRICS members Russia, India, China and South Africa. The "B" in BRICS stands for "Brazil" (B-Brazil, R-Russia, I-India, C-China & S-South Africa). In late September of 2015 President Dilma Rousseff gave her historic speech to the 70th U.N. General Assembly. It is as follows:

"..., Ladies and Gentlemen",

"It is my privilege to address the General Assembly in this year when the United Nations celebrates its seventieth birthday. Let my words Mr. President be to congratulate you for your appointment to preside over this Assembly. I reiterate in particular, Brazil's support for your efforts to adopt measures to strengthen the development agenda of this organization. Seventy years have passed since the San Francisco Conference. On the occasion the international community sought to build a world founded on International Law and on the peaceful resolution of conflicts. Since then there has been progress and setbacks. The decolonization process has shown notable evolution, as can be seen from the composition of this Assembly".

"The U.N. has broadened its initiatives, incorporating the 2030 Agenda and the Sustainable Development Goals, in other words, issues related to the environment, poverty eradication, social development and access to quality services. Matters such as urban challenges and gender and race issues have become a priority. The Organization has not had the same success though, in addressing collective security, an issue which was present at the U.N.'s origin and which remains at the center of its concerns. The proliferation of regional conflicts – some with high destructive potential – as well as the expansion of terrorism that kills men, women and children, destroys our heritage and displaces millions of people from their secular communities, shows the United Nations is before a great challenge".

"One cannot be complacent with barbaric acts such as those perpetrated by the so-called Islamic State and other associated groups. This situation explains to no large extent, the refugee crisis that humankind is currently experiencing. A significant portion of men, women and children who perilously venture the waters of the Mediterranean and painfully wander along the roads of Europe, come from the Middle East and North Africa, from countries which had their State institutions destroyed by military action undertaken in contravention of international law, thereby opening space for terrorism".

"The profound sense of indignation caused by the picture of a dead Syrian boy on the beaches of Turkey and by the news of the 71 people asphyxiated inside a truck in Austria, must be translated into unequivocal acts of solidarity. In a world where goods and capital data and ideas flow freely, it is absurd to impede the free flow of people. Brazil is a hosting country. We have received Syrians, Haitians, men and women from around the world, just as we sheltered over a century ago, millions of Europeans, Arabs and Asians. We are a multi-ethnic country where differences coexist".

"Mr. President this worrisome backdrop dictates that we reflect on the future of the United Nations and requires that we act decisively and swiftly. We need a U.N. that is capable of promoting sustainable international peace and of acting quickly and efficiently in situations of crisis, localized regional conflicts and any crimes against humanity. We can no longer delay for example, the creation of a Palestinian State, coexisting peacefully and harmoniously with Israel. In the same vein, the expansion of settlements in the occupied territories cannot be tolerated".

"A comprehensive reform of its structure is paramount in order to give the United Nations the centrality it is entitled to. The Security Council needs to be expanded in its permanent and non-permanent categories, to become more representative, legitimate and effective. Most member States do not want a decision on this matter to be postponed. We expect that the session which begins today enters into an historic point of the U.N. trajectory and that it yields concrete results of reforming organization".

"Our region where peace and democracy reign, welcomes the establishment of diplomatic relations with Cuba and the United States, putting an end to a dispute derived from the Cold War. We hope that this process will be completed with the end of the embargo against Cuba. We also welcome the recent agreement reached with Iran which will allow that country to develop nuclear energy for peaceful purposes and restore the hope of peace for the whole region".

"In the BRICS we have launched a New Development Bank which will assist in expanding trade and investment and possibly in achieving the Sustainable Development Goal".

"Mr. President the 2030 Agenda outlines the future we want. The 17 Sustainable Development Goals reaffirm the basic tenet of Rio + 20: it is possible to grow, include, preserve and protect. They establish universal goals and highlight the need for cooperation among peoples and a common path for humanity. This agenda requires global solidarity, a determination from each of us and a commitment to confront climate change, overcome poverty and guarantee opportunities".

"In Paris this upcoming December, we must strengthen the Climate Convention while fully implementing its provisions and respecting its principles. The obligations to be undertaken must be ambitious – including with regard to financial technological support to developing countries and small islands, in line with the principle of common, but differentiated responsibilities. Brazil is making a significant effort to reducing greenhouse gas emissions, without jeopardizing our development. We continue to diversify the renewable sources in our energy mix which is among the cleanest in the world. We are investing in low-carbon agriculture, reduced deforestation in the Amazonian region by 82% and our ambition will continue to guide our actions".

"In this spirit I announced yesterday here at the United Nations, our INDC (Intended Nationally Determined Contributions). Brazil's contribution will be a reduction of 43% of its greenhouse gas emissions by 2030, having 2005 as the base year. In this period, Brazil intends to put an end to illegal deforestation, to reforest 12 million hectares, to recover 15 million hectares of degraded pastures and to integrate 5 million hectares of crop – livestock – forests".

“In a world where renewable energy is only 13% of the energy mix, we intend to ensure a ratio of 45% of renewable sources in our energy mix. We will aim for a proportion of 66% of hydropower in our electricity generation output, a share of 23% of renewable resources, including wind, solar and biomass power in our electricity efficiency rate. Also a proportion of 16% of ethanol fuel and other sugarcane-derived biomass sources in our energy mix”.

“Brazil is thus contributing decisively to the global efforts towards implementing the recommendations on the Intergovernmental Panel on Climate Change, which has established the limit of no more than 2 degrees Celsius for global warming in this century. Brazil is one of the few developing countries to commit an absolute goal for emissions reduction. Our INDC include actions to increase the resilience of the environment and to reduce the risks associated with the negative effects of climate change on the poorest and most vulnerable populations, with an emphasis on gender issues, worker’s rights and the indigenous quilombola (Afro-Brazilian descendants) and traditional communities. We recognize the importance of South – South cooperation, in the global efforts to counter climate change”.

“I would emphasize that since 2003, social policies and conditional cash transfer programs have helped lift over 36 million people out of extreme poverty. Last year Brazil graduated from the World Hunger Map. This is a testament to the efficiency of our zero hunger policy, which has now become the SDG number 2. In transition to a low-carbon economy it is important to secure dignified and fair conditions for workers. Sustainable development requires us to commit to the promotion of decent work and the generation of quality jobs and opportunities. The efforts to eradicate poverty and promote development must be collective and global. In my country we know that the end of poverty is only the beginning of a long journey”.

"Mr. President, for a period of six years we sought to keep the impacts of the world crisis that emerged in 2008 in the developed world, from impacting our economy and our society. During these six years we adopted a comprehensive set of measures by lowering taxes, expanding credit, strengthening investment and stimulating household consumption".

"This effort reached its limits, due to both internal fiscal constraints and external conditions. A slow recovery of the world economy and the end of the commodities super cycle, negatively affected our economic growth. Currency devaluation and recessive pressures brought about inflation and a strong reduction in tax revenues, leading to restrictions on public finance. In order to face this situation we are rebalancing our budget and have strongly reduced public expenditures, including investments".

"We realigned prices and are adopting measures for permanent spending cuts, as well as limitations on credit incentives. We are also redefining sources of revenue. All of these initiatives aim to reorganize the fiscal situation and lower inflation, in order to consolidate macro-economic stability, increase confidence in the economy and ensure the resumption of economic growth with income distribution. The Brazilian economy is today stronger, more solid and resilient than some years ago. We are capable of overcoming the current difficulties, as we advance in our path towards development".

"We find ourselves at a moment of transition to another cycle of economic expansion, a profound solid and long-lasting one. In addition to the measures for fiscal and financial rebalancing and of incentives to exports, we also adopted measures to foster investments in infrastructure and energy. In Brazil the process of social inclusion has not been interrupted. We hope that the control of inflation, as well as the resumption of economic growth and credit, will contribute to further expansion of household consumption. There are the basis for a new development cycle led by an increase in productivity and the generation of more investment opportunities for businesses, as well as more jobs for citizens".

"Ladies and Gentlemen, our achievements through the last few years have been reached in an environment of consolidation democracy. Thanks to the efficiency of our legal system and to the strongest democratic institutions, the functioning of the State and impartially by the Judiciary and all the branches and public institutions in charge of supervising, investigating and punishing misconduct and crimes. Brazilian government and society do not tolerate corruption. The Brazilian democracy becomes stronger when the authorities recognize the limits imposed by the law, as their own limits. We Brazilians want a country where the law is the limit".

"Many of us fought for this precisely when laws and rights were violated during the military dictatorship. We want a country where rulers behave strictly according to their duties, without giving way to excesses. Where judges judge with freedom and impartiality, without any pressure whatsoever and disconnected from political passions, never compromising on the presumption of innocence of any citizen".

"We grant a country where the clash of ideas takes place, in a civilized, respectful environment. We want a country where freedom of the press is one of the cornerstones of the freedom of speech and the expression of different positions, a right of all Brazilians. The sanctions of the law must apply to all those who committed illicit acts, bearing in mind the need to uphold the principle of due process. These are the very foundations of our democracy, in this regard I avail myself of a recent statement made by my friend Jose' Mujica, former President of Uruguay, who quoted, 'This democracy is not perfect, for we are not perfect. However, we must defend it in order to improve it, not bury it! Let it be known that we will not relinquish the achievements for which the Brazilian population has greatly struggled".

"Ladies and Gentlemen, I would like to take this opportunity to reiterate that Brazil welcomes the citizens from around the world with open arms for the 2016 Olympic and Paralympic Games to be held in Rio de Janerio. This will be a unique opportunity to promote sports as a key tool for peace, social inclusion and tolerance and in the fight against racial, ethnic or gender discrimination. It will also be an opportunity to promote the rights and inclusion of persons with disabilities, one of the priorities of my government".

"One last point, a few days ago the murals of "War" and "Peace" by Brazilian artist Candido Portinari donated to the organization by the government of my country, in 1957, were re-inaugurated here at the United Nations headquarters. These works of art denounce violence and poverty and call upon peoples of the world to seek understanding and tolerance. They are a symbol representing the responsibility of the United Nations to prevent armed conflict and promote peace, social justice and the eradication of hunger and poverty. Portinari always said, 'There is no great art which is not identified with people'.

"The message of the murals remain valid. It alludes not only to the victim of wars, but to the refugees who risk their lives on fragile boats in the Mediterranean, as well as all the anonymous people who seek in the United Nations, protection, peace and well-being. We hope that upon entering the United Nations and gazing upon the murals, we may be capable of hearing the voices of the people we represent and of working persistently so that their calls for peace and progress may be heeded. These were after all, the ideals which were presented seventy years ago, at the foundation of this important accomplishment for humanity, namely the Organization of the United Nations. Thank You"!

In the months following this historic speech by such a worldly and wise stateswoman, in early December, 2015 front-men from the Israeli colony of the United States still persisted in attempting to get their hands on the Petrobra Oil Corporation. They quietly kept nudging Brazil's lower house president Eduardo Cunha to fast-track an impeachment process against President Dilma Rousseff on hastily trumped-up charges. Cunha, who himself was under investigation was seen at this juncture in time, to both be attempting to deflect the criminal focus surrounding himself onto the president, as well as to serve these Western destabilization agents and their oil-hungry bosses. Americans still yet remain indifferent and reluctant to prosecute the criminality within their own government and as one can see, the results are a contagion which is spreading around the world.

Mark my words, this great delay by America's citizens in someday attempting to finally take action in addressing its government's corruption, will be met with a very powerful force. Their time to take action is running out and their naive passivity is sentencing them to a life of ever greater and greater damnation. Once the day finally does arrive when they seek in demanding justice, if they have arrived too late it will be the spark that ignites the next Bolshevik-like Revolution. Inconceivable numbers of Americans will die unnecessarily, all because they chose for too long, to remain comfortably indifferent.

For Americans to do nothing and find themselves wrapped in the thumb-sucking solace of their sofa-blankets, seeking to find closure on one of their T.V. set's six major networks, the shear fact that what news companies they're watching are in obvious collusion with the very instigators they attempt to mentally escape, aborts closure into a false sense in peace-of-mind. They are no longer sitting in a home that is a self-expression of their freedom's accomplishments, taking pride in their achievements as a personal trophy. Rather, they are only continuing to live a deeper lullaby lie, as a prisoner in their own home

In June of 2015 a Reuters' investigation revealed that from 1996 to 2016, $8.5 trillion had been unaccounted for by the U.S. Pentagon's Budget Office. Had U.S. taxpayers demanded a refund of these funds to be at the very least, redistributed back into the Federal budget, plus the $2 trillion they reported had gone missing in 2001 to fund 9-11 and the start of the Iraq war, plus the total funds used in the 2008 bank bailouts, which alone correlated into $40,000 for-every-man-woman-and-child in America and had its citinzenry gave yet further "push-back" to have had The Federal Reserve relinquished, plus the funds from all the wars following Iraq, the United States citizens would today be enjoying a completely balanced buget. They would have also been rewarded with all their infrastructure having been completely refurbished and updated, a new free Apple Air pad for every child in America, free college tuition, free healthcare and a 3 and ½ day work week with ten hour days and no 2nd or 3rd shifts ever!

It is their profound apathy alone which is the biggest atrocity of humanity, since they are now the major funders of all terrorism in the world today, themselves.

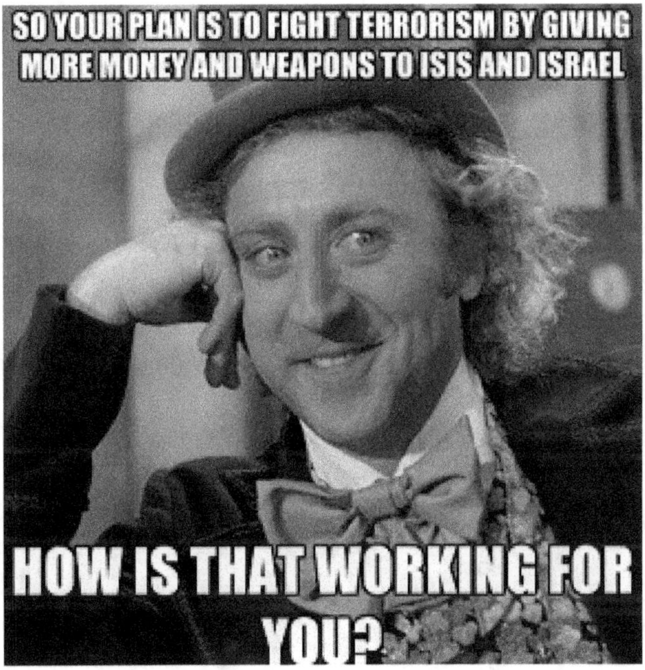

# Chapter III

## The Snow Leopard

"Russia's Diplomatic Weapon; meet Mr. Sergey V. Lavrov." Within the wheeling and dealing on the matters of Syria between the Russia Federation and the United States, can be found a most unique and highly seasoned Russian diplomat, Russian Foreign Minister Sergey Lavrov. I have this man as this chapter's subject matter in representing Russia, due to the fact that most of my previous book, "This is a Man 'A study of Vladimir Putin and our modern era", was devoted to Russia's President Valdimir Putin!

On the surface Mr. Lavrov has been profiled by many to come across as a bit of a James Bond-like character, reflected in his natural state as being rather debonair, known for giving flowers to female reporters and spending his recreational time either skiing, kayaking, drinking expensive scotch or smoking cigars. Nicknamed by some as "Minister Nyet" as his masterful ability in negotiations most often affords him an unwavering ability to get exactly what he wants, I hereby anoint him "The Snow Leopard".

Foreign Minister Lavrov served as the deputy head of the United Nations weapons inspectors program in Iraq, after the first Iraq war. This experience alone has left his counterpart, U.S. Secretary John Kerry very little wiggle room when it came to the dismantling of chemical weapons in Syria. What makes things enjoyable for many to read about Mr. Lavrov for Western readers, is how the likes of the New York Times chooses his descriptions; "Mr. Lavrov, a chain-smoker, is known as an old-school diplomat. He flatly ignored an effort by U.N. Secretary General Koti Annan to ban smoking in the United Nations headquarters, saying Mr. Annan did not own the building. He enjoys whiskey and cigars and his hobbies tend toward action sports like rafting and skiing".

In another matter, when a photographer asked Mr. Lavrov, Mr. Kerry and special envoy Lakhdar Brahimi to pose after a meeting in Geneva, Lavrov quipped, "You don't give orders, you just capture the moment". What is admired by me concerning this highly respectable character is exactly what he's so well regarded for in Russia's political circles; his natural ability to assume that whatever it is your thinking or asking for is completely irrelevant, as his style of diplomacy never uses handholding or pandering, but rather "hard talks" and articulate speech. While he leaves American politicians scrambling with their political correctness, Sergey Lavrov offers a very refreshing approach which is that he possess no fears to call things as he sees them.

Early in January of 2015 Foreign Minister Lavrov stated on Venezuelan State television; "The unipolar world has ceased to exist, now that powerful new centers of economic growth are emerging in Asia and Latin America. Old habits die hard. Parting with one's sense of global domination is not easy and this process is going to be long and painful, but I'm sure that in the long haul we'll agree on the need to redistribute our responsibilities from conflict resolution to economics, to finance and trade".

He also emphasized the need to end an outdated practice of using one country's laws on another's territory. Lavrov said, "All this should be done strictly in line with the U.N. Charter and without undermining the authority of the U.N. Security Council. We are against quick fixes here. All these problems should be tackled having fully in mind, the hard fact that global politics, economics and finance are no longer directed by a single center, that there are new, powerful centers of economic and financial growth now emerging in Asia and Latin America, adding political clout to these now, economic powerhouses".

Of the so-called "legal extraterritorial", Lavrov warned when unilateral sanctions are imposed in circumvention of the U.N. Security Council they are aimed at undermining a country's economic and social stability. "Economic ties, trade, technological exchanges, all this holds the key to development, while one-sided sanctions thwart the countries' pursuit to a better life", the Foreign Minister concluded.

On February 7, 2015, Russian Foreign Minister Sergey Lavrov delivered a speech at the Munich Security Conference. It was as follows;

"Ladies and Gentlemen,"

"Mr. Wolfgang Ischinger has included the issue of the collapse of global development on the agenda. One has to agree that events have taken a turn which is far from optimistic. But it is impossible to agree with the arguments of some of our colleagues, that there was a sudden, rapid collapse of the world order that had existed for decades".

"To the contrary, the last year's development confirmed the correctness of our warnings against profound, systematic changes in the organization of European security and international relations in general. I would like to remind you of the speech delivered by Russian President Vladimir Putin from these stands eight years ago".

"The structure of stability based on the U.N. Charter and the Helsinki principles has long been undermined by actions of the United States and its allies in Yugoslavia which was bombed, as well as in Iraq and Libya, NATO's expansion to the east and the creation of new lines of separation. The project of building a 'common European home' failed because our Western partners were guided by illusions and beliefs of winners in the Cold War, rather than the interests of building an open security architecture with mutual respects of interests. The obligations solemnly undertaken as part of the OSCE (Organization for the Security and Cooperation in Europe) and the Russian – NATO Council, not to ensure one's own safety at the expense of others, remained on paper and were ignored on practice".

"The problem of missile defense is vivid evidence of the powerful, destructive influence of unilateral steps in the development of military capabilities, contrary to lawful interests of other States. Our proposals on joint operation in the anti-missile field were rejected. In exchange we were advised to join the creation of a global U.S. missile defense, strictly according to Washington's templates which, as we underlined and explained, based on facts a number of times, carries real risks for the Russian nuclear deterrence forces".

"Any action undermining strategic stability will inevitably result in countermeasures. Thus, long-term damage is inflicted upon the entire system of international treaties dealing with control over armaments, the feasibility of which directly depends on the missile defense factor".

"We do not even understand what the United States' obsession with creating a global missile defense system can be connected with. With aspirations to indisputable military supremacy? With faith in the possibility to resolve issues are in reality political? In any case the missile threats did not become weaker, but a strong irritant emerged in the Euro-Atlantic region and it will take a long time to get rid of it. We are ready for this. Refusal of the United States and other NATO members to ratify the Agreement of Adaptation of the Treaty on Conventional Armed Forces in Europe, which buried this treaty, was another destabilizing factor".

"At the same time our U.S. colleagues are attempting to lay the blame on Russia in each complicated situation, they themselves created. Let's take the discussions which have revived recently on the Intermediate-Range Nuclear Forces Treaty (the INF Treaty). Specialists are well aware of the United States' actions which are in conflict with the spirit and the letter of this document. For instance, as part of the creation of a global missile defense system Washington commissioned a large-scale program of creating target missiles with characteristics similar, or close to land-based ballistic missiles, prohibited by the aforementioned treaty. Unmanned fighting vehicles widely utilized by the U.S., fall into the treaty's definition of intermediate-range cruise, land-based missiles. The treaty directly prohibits ABM launchers which will soon be deployed in Romania and Poland because they can be used to launch intermediate-range cruise missiles".

"While refusing to acknowledge these facts, our U.S. colleagues assert they have some 'substantiated' claims against Russia, with respect to the INF Treaty, but diligently avoid specifics. With due account of these and many other factors, attempts to narrow down the current crisis to last year's developments, to our mind, means falling into dangerous self-deception".

"There is a pinnacle in the course pursued by our Western colleagues in the past quarter of a century, on preserving their domination in the world affairs by all possible means, on seizing the geopolitical space in Europe. They demanded of the CIS countries (Commonwealth of Independent States) – our closest neighbors, connected with us by centuries economically, historically, culturally and even in terms of family ties – that they make a choice: 'either with the West, or against the West'. This is a zero-sum logic which ostensibly, everyone wanted to leave in the past".

"The strategic partnership of Russia and the European Union failed the test of strength, as the EU chose a path of confrontation over the development of mutually beneficial interaction mechanisms. We cannot help remembering the missed opportunity to implement Chancellor Merkel's initiative put forward in June 2010 in Meseberg, to create a EU-Russia Committee on Security and Foreign Affairs at the level of foreign ministries. Russia backed that idea, but the EU rejected it. Meanwhile, this constant dialogue mechanism, if it were to be set-up, would allow for solving problems faster and and more effectively and for resolving mutual concerns in a timely manner".

# UKRAINE CRISIS: JUST ANOTHER GLOBALIST-ENGINEERED POWDER KEG

f 38 29 0

**Brandon Smith**
alt-market.com
March 10, 2014

When one studies history, all events seem to revolve around the applications and degenerations of war. Great feats of human understanding, realization and enlightenment barely register in the mental footnotes of the average person. War is what we remember, idealize and aggrandize, which is why war is the tool most often exploited by oligarchy to distract the masses while it centralizes power.

"As for Ukraine itself, unfortunately at each stage of crisis development our American colleagues and their under influence, also the European Union, have been taking steps leading to escalation. This happened when the EU declined to involve Russia in the discussion of the consequences of implementing the economic block of the Association Agreement with Ukraine which followed by a direct support of a coup d'e tat and anti-government riots, prior to that. This also happened when our Western partners kept issuing indulgences to the Kiev authorities who, rather than keeping their promise to launch nation-wide dialogue, began a large-scale military operation and labelled 'terrorists', all citizens who defied the unconstitutional change of power and the rule of ultranationalists".

"It is very hard for us to explain why many of our colleagues fail to apply to Ukraine, the universal principles of settling internal conflicts with presuppose above all, an inclusive political dialogue between the propagandists. When do our partners, in the cases of Afghanistan, Libya, Iraq, Yemen, Mali and South Sudan for instance, urge the government to talk with the opposition, with rebels, in some cases, even extremists, whereas in the Ukraine crisis, our partners act differently, in fact, encouraging Kiev's military operation, going so far as to justify, or attempt to justify the use of cluster munitions".

"Regretfully, our Western colleagues are apt to close their eyes to everything that is said and done by Kiev authorities, including fanning xenophobic attitudes. Let me quote: 'Ukrainian social-nationalism regards the Ukrainian nation as a blood-race community'. Which is followed by: 'The issue of total Ukrainization in the future social nationalist State will be resolved within three to six months, by a tough and balanced State policy'. The author of those words is Andrey Biletsky, the commander of the Azov regiment, which is actually engaged in the military activities in Donbass. Some other activists who gained a position in politics and power, including Dmitry Yarosh, Oleg Tyagnibok and the leader of the Radical Party in the Verkhovna Rada, Oleg Lyashko, publically called a number of times for an ethically clean Ukraine, for the extermination of Russians and Jews. Those statements failed to evoke any reactions in the Western capitals. I don't think present day Europe can afford to neglect the danger of the spread of the neo-Nazi virus".

"The Ukrainian crisis cannot be solved by any military force. This was confirmed last summer when the situation on the battlefield forced the participants to sign the Minsk Accords. It is being confirmed now as well, when the next attempt to gain a military victory is failing. Yet regardless of all that, more loud calls are being made in some Western countries to step-up support of the Kiev authorities' vector towards militarization of society and the State, to 'infuse' Ukraine with lethal weapons, to drag it into NATO. There is hope in the increased opposition in Europe to such plans, which can only make the tragedy of the Ukraine people worse".

"Russia will continue to strive for establishing peace. We are consistently calling for the cessation of military activities, the withdrawal of heavy weapons and the start of direct talks between Kiev and Donetsk and Lugansk on practical steps to restore the common economic, social and political space within the territorial integrity of Ukraine. Numerous initiatives by President Putin were dedicated to exactly that, within the Normandy format which helped launch the Minsk process and our further efforts on the expansion, including yesterday's talks in the Kremlin between the Russian, German and French leaders. As you know, these talks are ongoing. We believe that there is every possibility we will reach results and agree on recommendations that will really allow the parties to untie the knot of this conflict".

"It is crucial that everyone should be aware of the real magnitude of the risks. It is high time we abandon the custom of considering every problem separately, unable to see the forest from the trees. It is time to give a comprehensive assessment of the situation. The world is now facing a drastic shift connected with the change of historic eras. The 'labor pains' of the new world structure are manifested in the increased proneness to conflicts in international relations. If short-sighted, practical decisions in the interests of the nearest elections at home will prevail with politicians, over a strategic, global vision, the risk will emerge of losing global management control".

"Let me remind you that at the onset of the Syrian conflict, many people in the West advised not to exaggerate the danger extremism and terrorism, stating that the danger would somehow dissipate by itself, while attaining a regime change in Damascus was a key priority. We see what has come out of it. Huge areas in the Middle East, in Africa, in Afghani-Pakistani area, are dropping out of legitimate government control. Extremism is spilling into other regions, including Europe. Risks of WMD proliferation are intensifying. The situation with the Middle East settlement and in other regional conflict areas is acquiring an explosive character. No adequate strategy on curbing those challenges has been worked out so far".

"I would like to hope that today's and tomorrow's debates in Munich will bring us closer to understanding the level of efforts on searching for collective answers to threats which are common for all. The talk, if we want a serious result, can only be equal, without ultimatums and threats. We are still confident that the overall complex of issues, could be resolved much more easily, if the largest players agreed on strategic landmarks in their relations".

"Recently Helen Carrere d' Encausse, prominent Secretary of the Academie Francise whom I hold in high esteem said, that a real Europe may not exist without Russia. We would like to see if this perspective is shared by our partners, or if they are inclined to keep deepening the split in common European space and setting its fragments in opposition to each other. Do they want to build a security architecture with Russia, without Russia, or against Russia? Of course, our American partners will have you answer to that question".

"We have long been proposing the creation of a common economic and humanitarian space from Lisbon to Vladivostk, based on the principles of equal and inseparable security that would encompass both members of integration unions and those nations that are not a part of them. Setting up reliable interaction mechanisms between the EAEU (Eurasian Economic Union) and the EU (European Union) is especially topical. We welcome the emerging support for this idea by responsible European leaders".

"On the $40^{th}$ anniversary of the Helsinki Final Act and the $25^{th}$ anniversary of the Charter of Paris, Russia calls for infusing documents with real life for preventing the substitution of principles they contain, for ensuring stability and prosperity in the whole of the Euro-Atlantic space, based on true equality, mutual respect and consideration for each other's interests. We wish success to the OSCE-formed "Group of Wise Men", which should reach a consensus in its recommendations".

"As we mark the $70^{th}$ anniversary of the end of WW II one should remember the responsibility each of us bears. Thank You for your attention"!

I felt this speech warranted a unique and historic example of one of the most astute and well-spoken Russian officials in foreign affairs today, Russian Foreign Minister, Sergey Lavrov. His words oftentimes even shame the West's best speech writers. Sergey Lavrov is not only a natural Russian at heart, but he knows very well "how to relate to Americans" and he certainly knows full well, how to act and relate to Europeans, because as a groundswell of critics have been saying all along, "Russia" is far more European at heart than the United States could ever hope to be.

In studying Mr. Lavrov I also noticed something that I could appreciate more in him than of many others. While doing a three year stint in South China I once served as a "mock-IELTS Examiner" (International English Language Testing System). I found that the key to a good speaker and in Mr. Lavrov's case, "a very strategic speaker", is to have the conditioned ability to steer the audience's route of thought just slightly off the road on either side, in just the precise amount as to make the conversation both interesting and entertaining, but not to a degree where you lose your driving theme in question home. Sergey Lavrov is a master of this craft which he often executes with much greater finesse than any of his counterparts.

Sergey Lavrov meticulously pin-points, exactly how and why the failure of the West's foreign policy agendas have transformed into a dishonorable, disgraceful, unlawful, inhumane, malicious, deceiving, corrupt and non-sustaining malignancy for the entire free and peace-loving world to see. For all his avant-garde, or even critical descriptions of him, Mr. Lavrov is himself, truly a man who cares from the heart and who is compassionately devoted, with every fiber in his makeup, to averting the dangers of the West's reckless and sadomasochistic captains at the wheel, who lust for domination, control and an ever greater and greater risk of blind Armeggedon.

In conclusion, Russia's Foreign Minister, Sergey Lavrov has caused a global consensus of the world's democracies' people to rise to the surface. In its final evaluation it is evidently clear that unanimously, globally and worldwide, "the people" of all nations are grossly weary of the world being held back by elitist, hyper-wealthy mad men who are hell-bent on disrupting the development of their lives and in trashing civilized and ethical progress. They have come to a point in time where they are all about to request to their leaders, the complete eradication of the world's current ruling classes, which they now see as being well worth its most revered prize and that is "world peace"!

# Chapter IV

## The BRICS Achilles's Heel

This chapter has proven to be most surprising. Though I support and favor in every way, the endeavors of the BRICS nations' successes in the multipolar perspective, I cannot in good conscience, support, nor trust "India" enough to be my partner in just about anything.

I have always had pleasant experiences and encounters with most all Indian people in my life however, and after completing my research of their country from almost every angle I discovered some surprising results. A persistent element to the study of India's Modi and Mukherjee policies in the contemporary sense, are ones which always seem to put "money" before all else, including ethics and justice. One can immediately notice that they've created a false representation by reflecting "their India" over the Indian peoples', portraying India to aspire to being "everyone's" friend; the BRICS, the U.K., the U.S.A., as well as Israel's.

Though it makes only good fellowship and fair and well-meaning diplomacy to hope, intend and aim for this all-inclusive goal to be in the warmest of relations with everyone, at the same time, one cannot have things both ways. By this I mean, for one to assume cozy and financially lucrative deals with countries whose intentions, agendas, policies and actions your people disagree with and whom might cause them harm, one is turning a blind eye, making a deal with the devil and "selling-out" their countrymen while deceptively insinuating it is possible to "trick God". Therefore, it is with these new, surprising findings I've unearthed concerning India's geopolitical posturing, that I am forced to anoint her "The BRICS Achilles' Heel" and would hope for a future replacement to the "I" in BRICS, perhaps by a nation more discreet, ethical and resistant to bribe, such as "Iran" perhaps.

Today's India demonstrates a considerable dose of political fence-sitting and two-timing. This nation has had much tighter bonds with Great Britain in its past than most would realize, even more so than that of Hong Kong. It continues a silent disdain for Pakistan and its Prime Minister is currently in a love affair with Israel and the U.S., which all bodes ill for India's Pakistani-China borders. Prime Minister Modi also appears to be in a lovefest with the concept of Facebook's mind-control, instead of hitting the pavement to lobby for new IT contracts for India's own IT industry. With much thanks to "Crook and Crook Inc." (Prime Minister Modi and President Mukherjee) India has now become a nation with the backbone of a cobra. Sounds rather harsh, but until the Indian government can produce a concrete stature with a conviction to foundational principles, ethics and morality and especially "loyalty", it cannot in fair conscience continue to talk sweetly from both sides of its mouth, while going to bed with nations who boycott

Russia, attempt to infiltrate South America, overthrow Syria, or restrain and destabilize the Muslim world and India's own farmers.

At this present juncture in time it would appear that India's government has been sold-out to America's Big Agri-business (Big Agra) and is destroying the self-sufficiency of its food products systems in the process. What highly lucrative market potential in the growing organic farming sector that Russia is successfully growing in by leaps and bounds, India's leaders are currently and abruptly tossing their identical opportunity down the toilet, in exchange for highly corrupt insider deals with folks like Monsanto and the use of GMOs. Another indicator to the India government's true identity which makes me apprehensive concerning their behavior as a major BRICS player is their overly cozy relationship with the unipolar players, especially "their military", both with the U.S. and Japan.

In September of 2015 the Indian military and U.S. Marines shared a 2 week training maneuvers for the 11th Itineration of Annual Exercises, in the Exercise Yudh Abhyas. Indian Army Lt. Colonel J.S. Ulshai, an officer with the Kumaon Regiment, commented from the activities: “Both armies have very common concerns, we have very similar interests...,”. The glaring indicator that India is blatantly behaving more like a poster child for the New World Order, than anyone to be trusted as a “member in good standing” within the BRICS’ coalition, was the following statement made offsite: “They want what we want,” said political scientist, Stephen Cohen, a senior fellow and India expert from the “Brookings Institute”. This exercise is just one part of an effort being made for the U.S. and India, in seeking closer ties. But the U.S. continuing operations in Central Asia, its increased presence in the Pacific Rim, militarily and its attempts to broaden its engagement in and around the South China Sea are all meant for predominantly one objective; “to sabre-rattle China”. I’m sorry, but I smell a rat here and I’m getting a clear signal India demonstrates no sense of unified loyalty to the BRICS, NATO or anyone else beyond money and money alone. Keep in mind too, that this comes from its current leadership and not necessarily the consensus of their peoples.

U.S. Army units based on the American West Coast, JBLM, home to the U.S. Army’s’ I-Corps, hosted training sessions which involved both Indian and Japanese troops. If one adds this to the man from Brookings, Mr. Cohen who further commented that New

Delhi is wary of Beijing's growing military strength, I for one see a two-faced BRICS member who has every intention of undermining the coalition. In May of 2016 India signs an accord with Russia and China supporting China's stance on the South China Sea, then hops over the other side of the fence to perform military maneuvers at sea with the U.S. and Japan, both within sixty days of one another.

Mr. Stephen Cohen from the Brookings Institute offered additional comments, saying there was, "..., financial incentives....," for the Indian military to take part in the missions.

The Brookings Institute originated the monetary programs implemented by the Federal Reserve System to destroy the American farmer, a replay of the Soviet era tragedy in Russia with one provision that the farmer would be permitted to survive, so long as he or she becomes a slave worker of the giant trusts. The Brookings Institute was incorporated by Franklin A. Delano, uncle to former U.S. President Franklin D. Roosevelt. Delano was on the original Board of Governors of the Federal Reserve System. The Delanos being foundational backers to the New World Order, trace their lineage directly back to William of Orange and the regime which granted the charter of the Bank of England. Brookings, as mentioned later in Chapter IX, has been telling the United States government how to conduct its affairs for the past 70 years and is still doing so today.

Gopalan Balachandran is a researcher at India's Institute for Defense Studies and Analysis. During an interview there seems an unspoken intention for India to increase and/or explore an opportunity to "open increased arms purchases with both Israel and the U.S.", while demonstrating a reluctance to rely on Moscow or Paris in the future. Balachandran stated: "With no outstanding political differences and with a growing economy, India presents opportunities to the U.S. business interests, both militarily and non-militarily. Hence, there is a move towards improving U.S.-India military ties, especially in military supplies and technology".

The further and deeper one studies India today, the more obvious and apparent it becomes that India's government has well sold-out to "the unipolar world" and shares no common interests with the BRICS nations today, worthy of any praise, mention or membership. And as one who's been around the geopolitical - alternative news scene for more than 12 years, I can safely say I'm all for expelling India from the BRICS coalition. Why? For openers, their government is in bed with the U.S. – Japan military, Monsanto, Big Agra-Biz, the IMF (international Monetary Fund), the World Bank, the Brookings Institute and Harvard University of the United States. Oh and did I fail to mention this little slimy tidbit; since 1997 "300,000 Indian farmers have committed suicide"!

Food and trade policy analyst Devinder Sharma, further describes the India predicament: "India is on a fast-track to bring agriculture under corporate control...,Amending the existing laws on land acquisition, water resources, seed, fertilizer, pesticides and food processing, the government is in overdrive to usher in contract farming and encourage organized retail. This is exactly as per the advice of the World Bank and the IMF, as well as international financial institutes".

In its 2008 World Development Report Sharma notes that the World Bank wanted India to hasten the process by accelerating land acquisitions while making younger people in rural areas more eligible for industrial work, through launching a network of training institutes. A highly contentious push to facilitate private corporations' access to land is actively underway, sparking mass protests across the country.

"U.S. subsidies and global trade policies", describes Sharma, "work to benefit huge, wealthy agribusiness corporations, crippling the poorer country's agricultural sectors in the process. Bucking markets in favor of Washington, lower global produce prices are caused by the massive subsidies doled out by the U.S. to giant agribusiness companies. In its usually corrupting fashion to keep out exports, the United States has also included non-trade barriers such as various health standards and regulations. At the same time, the Indian government is cutting its support for its own farmers, while further opening its markets to Western monopolies. With a global market slanted in favor of U.S. interests, outside Indian farmers are sentenced to walk-the-plank, while its political insiders line their pockets with perks, bribes and lucrative deals. In reality, the world is currently witnessing a once sovereign nation (India), sacrilegiously having its soul sold by its politicians, to the highest bidder, in the largest land rush of the century".

This "is not" a BRICS nation. It is rotten to the core and what's troubling BRICS investors is India's privilege to be situated near the BRICS own core. A GMO – BRICS? Not exactly a good selling point for attracting new investment capital!

What is happening courtesy of compliant politicians is tantamount to cannibalizing the country at the behest of foreign interests. Already gaining a foothold in India and its national public bodies, the West's Big Agra expands and grows its tentacles ever further. U.S. giants Cargill and Archer Daniels Midland are taking aim to completely reset India's entire rural communities. Picture what you can, what this will require; an economically forced exodus of 1 billion people to be transplanted into urban areas.

There's nothing miraculous about India's economy. Its level of corruption dwarfs anything to be found, even if one were to combine all the remaining BRICS nations together in contrast. A word of caution; when investing in the BRICS I'd do it "ex-India". Otherwise one might find themselves suddenly dropped into one of those new sinkholes created by its Western Big Agra giants. India's public regulatory bodies are now riddled with conflicts-of-interests and severely compromised decision-making processes over GMO concerns. This is evident by the shear fact that Monsanto already dominates its cotton industry while it increasingly and successfully attempts reshaping India's agro-policies.

To understand this mentality of "capture and exploit" requires an astute degree in higher learning. You take worthless U.S. taxpayer dollars to subsidize Big Agra and rig the commodities markets at the further expense of destroying and uprooting foreign farmers. This felonious form of short-sighted gluttony is exemplified by the neoliberal APCO Worldwide Corporation, an organization that none other than Narendra Modi, India's own Prime Minister is closely associated with.

With more than 600 employees and 35 locations globally, APCO Worldwide is an independent global affairs and strategic communications consultancy which is also the second largest, independently owned PR firm in the U.S. It was founded by Margery Kraus in 1984 and is headquartered in Washington D.C. Relations Media outlet "Everything-PR" describes APCO as "one of the world's most powerful P.R. firms. Upon close examination it becomes quickly evident the firm specializes in coming to the rescue of corporate giants such as Phillip Morris, Merck, Hewlett Packard, WorldCom and others, who are in dire need of emergency window-dressing and "legal" cover-ups of flammable evidence which might ignite bad publicity.

In 1999 APCO Worldwide created the "One Israel" concept for Israeli Prime Minister Ehud Barak. In 2010 APCO was at the center of an Hewlett Packard scandal when its then CEO, Mark Hurd was exposed for using company funds to have an affair with ex-soft porn actress Jodie Foster.

Thus, India's Prime Minister Narendra Modi, is India's chauffeur on its last ride to hell, incapable and too belligerent to strengthen any working economy which should support his people. There's nothing awesome, or special about "selling out" at the expense of your own countrymen. As he watches with a stupid-faced grin, corporate monopolies are hollowing out what took his country's people generations to build. He knows full well that after he and all his insider cronies have made their riches that India will be sentenced to 20-45% unemployment rates. In ten years the corporate rape will have passed and much like the devastation and despair once left behind Margret Thatcher, Modi will be hiding somewhere in the Caymen Islands, puffing on expensive cigars and drinking the vintage blood wines from the land he once came from and destroyed.

Believe it or not, this man actually has an accomplice who's equally as vile and corrupt, if not more so. That would be India's President Pranab Mukherjee which I have devoted the entire Chapter VIII to, coming up here later!

# Chapter V

## The West's Media Brainwash

Many in the West who are beginning to awaken from their overdosed stupors of one too many Taylor Swift videos while being MTV'd with in-your-face, gang'sta-rap escapades as they journey through the Matrix, just might be asking themselves how is it that with such alarming levels of heightened and permissive corruption going down on both Capitol Hill and Wall Street, can things yet remain so passive? An increasing number of Americans and Europeans are openly beginning to question the control of mind-numbing corporate media propaganda, given the increasingly blatant manner in which their ruling elites bluntly partake in open acts of corruption and malice, manifested from within a convoluted intertwine of government and corporate collusion.

Would someone please change the video game and tell them why aren't hundreds of thousands of people protesting in Frankfort, or Rome, in London or Brussels, or in Washington D.C., week after week? The paper-cut masses still frolic around thinking they're living in a free society, while some sort of mind-controlling gullibility projects them into a B-rated science-fiction flick, in drone-like automations as cooperative, zombie-humanoid robots.

Carefully planted deep within their collective psyche there lies a surrendering acceptance which wasn't there before and was not introduced by them themselves, but rather by a mind tenderizing propaganda phenomena which is beginning to befuddle, if not startle, more and more of those who are still with a sound mind. A spider-entity formed by collusion of a corporate-government, crime-meld keeps softly stroking these subjects' neuro-endings, as it successfully manipulates an acceptance of undemocratic practices, spun over a very crowded and distracting media backdrop which can cause permanent damage.

In a simpler context, current Western now media projects that all that is required for a happy life is to "not question" anything or anybody and simply kickback and relax, because they're your friend now and everything is just fine. You needn't ever concern yourself about anything in government, or big business anymore because they will do all that for you now, made clearly evident by the behind-closed-doors TIPP Trade Agreement. "Just go to work and have fun; leave the worrying to us".

Herein, any kid with even a C-average in history can tell you this spells Mommy and Daddy are on a slow boat to Fascism. Some calling it a prelude to a New World Order creep, it is as if you're riding a stagecoach and the highway robbers kill the driver and stop the stage. They open the doors and take all your money, then close the doors, mount the stage and proceed to take you to an unknown destination. If you remain on that stage, you will have just put all your faith in the highway robbers, that you and everything will be o.k. This is the "age of pioneering" on a road to hell. Western non-mainstream discussions are pointing to the rising dangers of a generalized mind-control acceptance as it ever increases the likelihood of the West becoming one big North Korea. Once

Western civilization is rendered totally passive, it is being warned that its Corporatocracy will then receive immediate incentive to crank up the flames of an oppressive regime, as it transforms the Western landscape into an advanced technocratic, surveilling, Fascist State. One that would pale in comparison to the Spanish Inquisition, since it will render all subjects total and complete digital slaves, with no exits and no alternatives. Yet out on the streets of the West there isn't a peep of protest.

It is time to take heed. In the Western unipolar world, making yourself a Christian, a Buddhist, a Hindi, a Moslem, or an atheist still offers no protection from the onslaught of this homogenized fusion of corporate and political evil. Even Eastern Europe where 7 out of 8 oligarchs of its most powerful crime syndicates are Zionist Jews, posing a threat to even the multipolar citizenry which lives there, the now Neo-Nazi Ukraine being its starkest example.

But the biggest threat of all is the surrendering to it, "especially" in its early stages when there still remains many open windows to hope. The entire populations of the Western unipolar society has succumbed to brainwashing for decades. The only truth they know was conveniently provided for them via mainstream media, where they were told what to wear, what to eat, how their children should be raised, how to run on emotions over logic and listen to hype and innuendo, over truthful facts. Their perceptions were swayed, massaged and manipulated in how they would conduct themselves in relationships, their approach to sex, the manners in which they talk, as well as their religious and political persuasions. Their mainstream mass media and Freudian social engineering have fed all this mentioned programming into their public consciousness.

To act on their own free will no longer seems to get them very far or much of any results, since they don't realize that the influence of a few powerbrokers have manipulated their "free will" into convincing them they are acting upon it, when they are only rolling over to play dead with smiles on their faces. Though the following individuals are only responsible for a percentage of this damage, the Zionist names Levin, Eisner, Bronfman, Redstone, Dammerman and Cherin now control 90% of the media, print, music and motion picture industry in American alone, through NewsCorp, GE, Viacom, Seagrams, Disney and Time Warner.

One can already witness some of the tell-tale signs that America is being transformed into Newmerika as it slowly begins evermore resembling Kim Jun Un's Republic of North Korea. This is more noticeable now in the disintegration of families, where say an older brother who maybe uses only internet alternative news programming, will be treated differently within a family. The mother of this son might blurt out occasionally, "don't listen to your brother Johnny, he only gets his opinions from those foreign wingnut, tinfoil hat survivalists on the internet". Sadly, though the mother can still see the humor in her words, she doesn't realize that in less than ten years the oligopolistic Corporatocracy she is defending, will likely come to extract Johnny as a "dissident" and take him to that same unknown destination as that stagecoach I mentioned earlier.

The fact that most people are totally unaware of the level of manipulation by the propaganda they are being subjected to, is the most pernicious effect of this all. It is nearing the time when we will be forced to treat and address the Western internet as one-in-the-same manner as its television programming, since the collusion of government and big industry was last seen preparing to apply their controls there, as well. The Western public will increasingly be manipulated, brainwashed and subconsciously controlled to believe the most outlandish lies which, given the lopsidedness of its points of origin being Zionist, will be inundated with anti-Muslim, anti-Russia, anti-China, anti-BRICS, anti-peace, anti-thought and anti-freedom propaganda and rhetoric.

As the doors of perception for Western civilization are slowing closing, there still exits even in its passive state, one last great chance to be rescued by awareness. Once the West's power-elite's agenda is imposed their citizen's doors of perception will step by step, slowly close and be altered through their vantage points within the internet via Network Neutrality, I.D. Systems and web bot spiders that will scour for key word strokes. "Dissident Extraction" will be rolled out into the open, as part of its new legal system and violators will be picked up routinely by GPS. The West's Corporatocracy wishes to put an end to their subject's free expression and accessibility to the truth. It now seeks to end all

independent thought and to muffle the last remaining forms of alternative, independent news reporting currently being made available to them.

The U.S. and Europe existing as two large North Koreas is not as far off as their masses realize. The majority of their male populations have already been well alienated and marginalized.

Over time, the people there will partake in little of any conversation and the bustling streets and sidewalks will gradually turn desolate. Its citizens will be judged and weighed on the scales of digital profiling and nothing, but nothing in their lives will ever be made a secret, or held sacred again; not their medical history, their fiscal balances, their personal persuasions, their tastes, buying habits or preferences, including intimate relations and associations. Actually, the West could say their 90% of the way there already. The citizen will receive stiff fines, or even jail sentences for not having a photo of the president in their home and "thought police" will profess to anticipate crime and offenses before they supposedly are to occur.

"Bad consumers" (those who don't spend enough each month) will have fines automatically withdrawn from their accounts and the outside worlds headlines in multipolar nations will carry horrifying stories of various pockets of starvation, famine and desperate massacres and plights of the planet's new American, Canadian, British and EU refugees. To be shot in back by Zionist Gestapos for attempting to flee the country will become commonplace. Each time one jaywalks, litters, spits, chews gum, speeds or runs a red light, algorithmic FRS devices (Facial Recognition Systems) will instantly deduct fines from your account. Delinquent account holders will see a rebirth to debtor's prisons and a rebirth in slave labor programs, to aid citizens in working their way back to “model status” and release.

If anyone reading this has a friend in a unipolar nation, do they really just wish to sit there and permit this type of a life to unfold? When things reach the point of boiling riots and Marshall Law, one has already passed the point of any hope in making a difference. So this begs an obvious question as to why it is there’s no massive groundswell in protests against Western institutions of control occurring? At best this can only serve as a free education to multipolar observers as to how to fortify every precautionary measure to their mortar. In learning how to prevent Western ills and to protect their existing systems from these decadent scenarios.

The majority of people awakened and aware of the present level of tyranny occurring, yet still seeming to be passive about it, can be explained by one psychological factor. A psychosis known as “Bystander Apathy” is predominantly factored into this behavioral equation, as the cause for deficient motivation. This phenomena refers to any scenario where the greater the number of people which are present, the less likely it is a person in distress will be rescued.

A psychological textbook example of Bystander Apathy can be studied in the case history surrounding the brutal murder of Catherine Genovese. In 1964, on March 13 the 28 year old woman was returning home after work. While she approached her apartment's entrance, she was repeatedly attacked and stabbed by a man the police later identified as Winston Mosley. Not one of the twelve people in the neighboring apartments answered Ms. Genovese's repeated screams for help, who later admitted having heard her cries. As the police investigation progressed it was later discovered that there was actually "38 witnesses" to the crime, all total. This preventable death began at 3:20 AM, yet the police were not first contacted until 3:50 AM. The failure of her neighbors to report this crime-in-progress gave rise to the term, "Bystander Apathy" and brought into Western national culture, a new dimension of human behavioral studies, concerning people's unwillingness to act in emergency situations.

Contributing to the psychosis there are two major factors. "Diffusion of responsibility" is one, first caused by the presence of other people. It was discovered that since the responsibility to take action was perceived to be shared among all present, the individuals did not feel as pressured to take action. Researchers concluded that the greater the number of people present generally speaking, renders a less likely chance of people taking action.

The second contributing factor to this mass psychosis researchers found, was the “need to behave in correct and socially acceptable ways”. Obviously the moral fiber in Western culture had dwindled to new lows, even fifty years ago. Individuals receive a signal from other observers failing to act that either “a response is not necessary” or that “it is not appropriate”. If the situation is ambiguous, it has been interpreted that they are less likely to act. Most of the 38 witnesses involved in the Genovese case reported that they did not realize the woman was being murdered and they assumed they were witnessing a “lover’s quarrel”. This is no different than saying, “Stalin’s Jewish death squads were just taking the Kulaks for a picnic in the country, of which they likely deserved”.

For either any awakened Western soul reading this, or the majority of the free and morally sane world outside its boundaries, “Bystander Apathy” signals a civilizations entrance into a phase of “National Suicide”, a precursor to an Empire’s last evolutionary stage, “the age of Decline and Fall”.

# Chapter VI

## The Quiet Tiger

A simple, yet powerful vision has been projected by China's President Xi Jinping. To instill a political and loyal union domestically while invoking influence abroad, he churns up a patriotic inspiration within the Chinese people by reverently bridging its ancient past to the bullet train speed of its future. Upon taking the helm of his presidency he successfully impressed the rest of the world and his domestic front, that he is a sound and highly capable leader with vast proportions of inner compassion that fuels his transformative agenda and perpetuates a reformation of China's political and economic relations.

At a moment in time when the economic success of his country was politically lost, he quickly took ownership of it with a constant drive and urgency in the assumption of his power. His style has been most unique among all China's leaders in that he rejected the old guard of traditional, collective leadership establishing himself as a more authentic leader himself, within the confines of a centralized system. His economic reforms are both smart and fruitful and while attacking corruption with a vengeance, he championed in something no other leader in all of Asia including Japan, has ever attempted since Genghis Khan; he promoted and encouraged "innovation". This has proven to be far more important and instrumental than outside observers might realize, since it completely shattered the old Sino-mold of being "just another copy-cat" while it creates something desperately needed in the contemporary mindset of global economics, something the Rockefellers have always been severely fearful of, "competition".

President Xi's consciousness proves him to be one of the wisest world leaders to ever walk onto the geopolitical stage, with an innate principle that an open door to Western eco-political ideas will undermine the validity and strength of China's culture. From a strategic point of view China has enjoyed few adversaries, as Australia and yes even Japan, now favor her business. Behind China's back only three nations bear a noteworthy surveillance; India, Israel and the Unites States. It is of worthy mention that in the comparison of President Xi to Western leaders, he immediately impresses as being a breed apart as he projects a pragmatic, yet potent energy of being genuinely authentic with no entities pulling his strings. He stands tall in his own brand of leadership and he always succeeds in captivating his constituency's interests because it is clearly evident he is not just a talking head.

The U.S. Council on Foreign Relations and its affiliate institutions have been sighted going through flips and twists, as all the major disturbances they have had a hand in creating, from Libya, Myanmar and North Korea, to Syria, and failed uprisings in Hong Kong, have proven to have been unsuccessful in luring China into becoming bogged down militarily, or destabilized domestically. Xi's policies have withstood well, the many Western pranks attempting to divide him from his grass roots base. The West now being a complete hostage to an Israeli-Rothschild criminal elite, still yet unchecked by it citizenry, continues to become forever confused and bewildered as to why Xi's political crackdowns and anti-corruption campaigns have strengthened his relations with resourceful Chinese. If some Chinese millionaires have chosen to leave, then they are the ones China is better off without! More Chinese are returning to China today, than are leaving it. The world has taken notice of a grave change in the West, one that they do not like. America once emulated, is now with few freedoms, no free trade or markets and has become lawless and a major human rights violator in the global arena while escalating to the levels of State-sponsored terrorism. It has now become evident to all geopolitical players that Israel has made the Unites States a limp puppet.

Today America's word and even its signatures on treaties mean next to nothing in most nations of our current times. Within the global all world leaders have woken up to the Zionist West's loss of credibility, its master's infatuation for destruction, manufactured terror and its lust for war. So it only stands to reason that any improvements China can make during this period will only double in value when put in comparison objectively, alongside the West of today. The world now craves for naturally respectable leadership and not the force-fed domination practices the West's Jewish terrorists assume!

On September 28, 2015 President Xi Jinping gave his first United Nations address. It is as follows:

"Mr. President, Dear Colleagues",

"Seventy years ago the earlier generation of mankind fought heroically and secured the victory of the World Anti-Fascist War, closing a dark page in the annals of human history. That victory was hard won. Seventy years ago the earlier generation of mankind with vison and foresight, established the United Nations. This universal and most representative and authoritative, international organization has carried mankind's hope for a better future and ushered in a new era of cooperation. It was a pioneering initiative never undertaken before".

"Seventy years ago the earlier generation of mankind pooled together their wisdom and adopted the Charter of the United Nations, laying the cornerstone of the contemporary order and establishing the fundamental principles of contemporary relations. This was an achievement of profound impact".

Mr. President, Dear Colleagues,"

"On the third of September the Chinese people with the world's people, solemnly commemorated the 70th Anniversary of the victory of the Chinese people's War of Resistance Against Japanese Aggression and the World Anti-Fascist War. As the main theatre in the East, China made a national sacrifice of 35 million causalities in its fight against the majority troops of Japanese militarism. It not only saved itself and its people from subjugation, but also gave support to the forces against aggression in the European and Pacific theatres, thus making a historic contribution to the victory of the World Anti-Fascist War".

"History is a mirror. Only by drawing lessons from history can the world avoid repeating past calamity. We should view history with awe and human conscience. The past cannot be changed, but the future can be shaped. Bearing history in mind is not to perpetuate hatred. Rather, it is for mankind not to forget its lesson. Remembering history does not mean being obsessed with the past. Rather, in doing so we aim to create a better future and pass the torch of peace from generation to generation".

(New Chinese fighter jet)

"Mr. President, Dear Colleagues,"

"The United Nations has gone through the test of time over the past seven decades. It has witnessed efforts made by all countries to uphold peace, build homeland and pursue cooperation. Having reached a new historical starting point, the United Nations needs to address the control issue of how to better promote world peace and development in the 21st century".

The world is going through an historic process of accelerated evolution: the sunshine of peace, development and progress will be powerful enough to penetrate the clouds of war, poverty and backwardness. The movement towards a multipolar world and the rise of emerging markets and developing countries, have become an irresistible trend of history. Economic globalization and the advent of the information age have vastly unleased and boosted social productive forces. They have both created the unprecedented development opportunities and given rise to new threats and challenges we must face squarely".

"As an ancient Chinese adage goes, 'the greatest ideal is to create a world truly shared by all'. Peace, development, equity, justice, democracy and freedom are common values of all mankind and lofty goals of the United Nations. Yet these goals are far from being achieved and we must continue our endeavor to meet them. In today's world all countries are interdependent and share a common future. We should renew our commitment to the purposes and principles of the U.N. Charter, build a new type of international relations featuring win-win cooperation and create a community of a shared future for mankind. To achieve this goal we need to make the following efforts":

- "We should build partnerships in which countries treat each other as equals, engage in mutual consultation and show mutual understanding. The principle of sovereign equality underpins the U.N. Charter. The future of the world must be shaped by all countries. All countries are equals. The big, strong and rich should not bully the small, weak and poor. The principle of sovereignty not only means that the sovereignty and territorial integrity of all countries are inviolable, but that their internal affairs are not subjected to interference".

- “We should be committed to multilateralism and reject unilateralism. We should adopt a new vision of seeking win-win outcomes for all and reject the outdated mindset that one’s gain means the other’s loss, or that the winner should take all. Consultation is an important form of democracy and it should also become an important means of exercising contemporary, international governance. We should resolve disputes and differences through dialogue and consultation. We should forge a global partnership at both international and regional levels and embrace a new approach to state-to-state relations, one that features dialogue rather than confrontation and seeks partnership rather than alliance. Major countries should follow the principles of no conflict, no confrontation and mutual respect and win-win cooperation in handling their relations. Big countries should treat small countries as equals and take a right approach to justice and interests by putting justice before interests”.

- “We should create a security architecture featuring fairness, justice, joint contribution and shared benefits. The age of economic globalization, the security of all countries, is interlinked and has impact on one another. No country can maintain absolute security with its own effort and no country can achieve stability out of other countries instability. The law of the jungle leaves the weak at the mercy of the strong; it is not the way for countries to conduct their relations. Those that adopt the high-handed approach of using force, will find that they are only lifting a rock to drop on their own feet”.

- “We should abandon Cold War mentality in all manifestation and foster a new vision of common, comprehensive cooperation, cooperative and sustainable security. We should give full play to the central role of the United Nations and its Security Council in ending conflict and keeping peace and adopt the dual approach of seeking peaceful solutions to disputes and taking mandatory actions, so as to turn hostility into amity. We should advance international cooperation in both economic and social fields and take a holistic approach to addressing traditional and non-traditional security threats, so as to prevent conflicts from breaking out in the first place".

- "We should promote open, innovative and inclusive development that benefits all. The 2008 international financial crisis has taught us that allowing capital to blindly pursue profit, can only create a crisis and that global prosperity cannot be built on the shaky foundation of a market without moral constraints. The growing gap between rich and poor is both unsustainable and unfair. It is important for us to use both the invisible hand and the visible hand to form synergy between market forces and government function and strive to achieve both efficiency and fairness".

"Development is meaningful only when it is inclusive and sustainable. To achieve such development requires openness and mutual assistance and win-win cooperation. In the world today, close to 800 million people still live in extreme poverty, nearly six million kids die before the age of five each year and nearly 60 million children are unable to go to school. The just concluded U.N. Sustainable Development Summit adopted the post 2015 Development Agenda. We must translate our commitments into actions and work together to ensure that everyone is free from want, has access to development and lives with dignity".

- "We should increase inter-civilization exchanges to promote harmony, inclusiveness and respect for differences. The world is simply more colorful as a result of its cultural diversity. Diversity breed exchanges, creates integration and makes progress possible".

"Within their interactions, civilizations must accept their difference. Only through mutual respect, mutual learning and harmonious coexistence, can the world maintain its diversity and thrive. Each civilization represents the unique vision and contribution of its people and no civilization is superior to others. Different civilizations should have dialogue and exchanges, instead of trying to exclude or replace each other. The history of mankind is a process of active exchanges, interactions and integration among different civilizations. We should respect all civilizations and treat each other as equals. We should draw inspirations from each other to boost the creative development of human civilization".

- "We should build an ecosystem that puts Mother Nature and green development first. Mankind may utilize nature and even try to transform it, but we are after all, a part of nature. We should care for nature and not place ourselves above it. We should reconcile industrial development with nature and pursue harmony between man and nature to achieve sustainable development of the world and the all-around development of man".

“To build a sound ecology is vital for mankind’s future. All members of the international community should work together to build a sound global, eco-environment. We should respect nature, follow nature’s ways and protect nature. We should firmly pursue green, low-carbon, circular and sustainable development. China will shoulder its share of responsibility and continue to play its part in this common endeavor. We also urge developed countries to fulfill their historic responsibility, honor their emission reduction commitments and help developing countries mitigate and adapt to climate change”.

“Mr. President, Dear Colleagues,”

“The over 1.3 billion Chinese people are endeavoring to realize the Chinese dream of great, national renewal. The dream of the Chinese people is closely connected with the dreams of other peoples of the world. We cannot realize the Chinese dream without a peaceful international environment, a stable international order and the understanding, support and help from the rest of the world.

The realization of the Chinese Dream will bring more opportunities to other countries and contribute to global peace and development. China will continue to participate in building a world of peace. We are committed to the peaceful development. No matter how the international landscape may evolve and how strong it may become, China will never pursue hegemony, expansion or sphere of influence".

"China will continue to contribute to global development. We will continue to pursue the common development of the win-win strategy of opening up. We are ready to share our development experience and opportunities with other countries and welcome them to board the China express train of development so that all of us will achieve common development".

"China will continue to uphold the international order. We will stay committed to the path of development through cooperation. China was the first country to put its signature on the U.N. Charter. We will continue to uphold the international order and system underpinned by the purposes and principles of the U.N. Charter. China will continue to stand together with other developing countries, especially African countries in the international governance system. China's vote in the United Nations will always belong to the developing countries".

"I wish to take this opportunity to announced China's decision to establish a 10 year, $1 billion China-U.N. peace and development fund to support the U.N.'s work, advance multilateral cooperation and contribute more to world peace and development. I wish to announce that China will join the new U.N. Peacekeeping Capability Readiness System and has thus decided to take the lead in setting up a permanent peacekeeping police squad and build a peacekeeping standby force of 8,000 troops. I also wish to announce that China will provide a total of $100 million of free military assistance to the African Union in the next five years, to support the establishment of the African Standby Force and the African Capacity for Immediate Response to Crisis".

"Mr. President, Dear Colleagues,"

"As the United Nations enters a new decade, let us unite evermore closely to forge a new partnership of win-win cooperation and a community of a shared future for mankind. Let the vision of a world free of war and with lasting peace take root in our hearts. Let the aspirations of development, prosperity, fairness and justice spread across the world! Thank You"!

President Xi Jinping overtook U.S. President Obama in the number of countries visited in 2015. The U.S. president having visited 11 countries, while Xi visited 14. To the extremist degree, France's president may very well be facing the guillotine once the French populace realizes their president extremely abused his position in visiting more than 50, China's President Xi has been the best travelled leader in the Communist Party's history. For 2015 he visited South Africa, Zimbabwe, France, Turkey, the Philippines, Singapore, Vietnam, Britain, U.S., Belarus, Russia, Kazakhstan, Indonesia and Pakistan.

Xie Tao, a professor of international relations at Beijing's Foreign Studies University stated, Xi is absolutely a high profile foreign policy president. Rather than only bringing in contracts for Chinese enterprises, Xi wants to gain more political influence abroad". An expert on Beijing's foreign policy, Mr. William Lam, from the Chinese University of Hong Kong says, "When China's internal economic growth is slowing down, Xi and the Communist Party have to show the Chinese people that China is playing a bigger role externally. I don't see a physical war between China and the U.S. in the near future, but the competition between the two countries will definitely grow more and more fierce".

To rival those of the West, Xi has developed several high-profile institutions which signal that his ambitions stretch well beyond just the next few years. His Beijing-based alternative to the World Bank, a multi-billion dollar Asian Infrastructure Investment Bank (AIIB) has attracted U.S. allies as founding members. Xi's plans to establish trade routes throughout Asia and Europe, through his One Belt, One Road initiative is an ambitious development strategy. Worth more than the total gross domestic product (GDP) of many small nations, while abroad for 2015 President Xi has signed $178 billion in business deals, including $7.7 billion with the French city of Toulouse, 70 commercial passenger planes with Airbus, a $5 billion deal to build a high-speed rail line connecting Los Angeles and Las Vegas and a $3 billion deal to build two "ecological parks" in Wales.

(China resurrecting islands in South China Sea)

Complimenting those deal-signings, Mr. Xi has aggressively reaffirmed China's land claims within the maritime territories of the Philippines, Brunei, Malaysia, Vietnam and Japan. Foreign Leaders have taken note of President Xi's unusually powerful position, as he is being called the strongest Chinese leader since Mao Zedong. Professor of International Relations at Renmin University of China in Beijing said, “In the era of Hu other countries sometimes weren’t so sure whether to listen to Hu or China’s Foreign Minister, especially when the two weren’t in perfect consensus. But everyone now knows if you want to deal with China, you need to deal with Xi Jinping”!

# Chapter VII

## The Firm Disciplinarian

This chapter was my second surprise in writing about the BRICS member nations. After a careful study of South Africa's President Zuma, I cannot in good faith write about either as it would take another book entirely. His six wives, a fiancé, plus two or three additional outside women, his estimated 20 to 25 children and a history of corruption that would fill an additional encyclopedia edition, leaves me only with a sobering inspiration to grant President Zuma my stiff stamp of rejection and a swift kick-to-the-curb. You can't make a silk purse from a sow's ear. So I hereby choose to replace "South Africa" and their president, with one of the BRICS competing "Next Eleven" countries, Nigeria and its president, President Muhammadu Buhari. He is the epitome of what both India and South Africa desperately need in leadership and he's also finding himself in the middle of having to rise to the greatest challenge of any other world leader today, including Yemen.

The new president of Africa's largest economy was once a military dictator, Muhammad Buhari. Being very popular in the north, Buhari was the strongest rival of incumbent Goodluck Jonathan. Northern Nigerians describe Buhari as a former general who's as incorruptible as they come and a stickler for discipline. The 72 year old quickly rose up the hierarchy after completing his military training and was awarded lucrative political posts which military rulers granted him. Having supported the introduction of Islamic Sharia Law in the north, he was regarded as a devout Muslim. From January 1984 until August of 1985, Buhari led the country following a successful coup. A war against "a lack of discipline" was his proclamation. Almost 500 people were jailed for corruption and there was no wasting taxpayer's money during his rule.

Witnesses reported State employees had to perform deep-knee bends if they came to work late. Buhari still lives in a modest house to this day and unlike most Nigerian politicians, he has not brazenly enriched himself. As is the case with most "former" dictators, Muhammadu Buhari once had a dark side. He was once deaf to calls for a transition to a more democratically legitimized government, had harassed the media and once had people executed. He once gave Nigerians the feeling they were living under an inflexible regime which spread fear, according to Nobel laureate Wole Soyinka.

Soyinka's daughter-in-law, Lola Shoneyin commented, "Things have changed. We have our courts now, we have a very active and vibrant civil society and we have the National Assembly.

A lot of things that might have been possible thirty years ago, in terms of corruption, just aren't possible now". Buhari tried to play down his controversial past during his campaign. Since an increasing number of Nigerians had the impression that outgoing President Goodluck Jonathan chose to just sit out the country's problems rather than tackle them head on, Buhari has profited from his hardliner image.

During a pre-election rally in Kano Buhari voiced general concern of the extent of corruption: "..., the lack of concern by the government for anything other than the retention of power at all costs". He also voiced further complaints of the poor security situation in the country and of the "scandalous level of unemployment" for millions of young Nigerians. Bearing all the Hallmarks of Boko Harem, Buhari's convoy was attacked in the city of Kaduna in June 2014. He has repeatedly said he would destroy the extremist group.

In March 2015 Buhari ran against a president from a ruling People's Democratic Party (PDP) after failed attempts in 2003, 2007 and 2011. What greatly increased the chances of his final victory were plainly due to the fact that it was the first time he had joined forces with the All Progressives' Congress (APC) and with several influential politicians, in order to win the necessary votes of the Christian dominated South. This constituency will likely modify his approach in how he fights corruption. Though his victory was secure, Buhari's shoulders' are laden with burden.

The "Next Eleven" nations (also referred to as N-11) are the countries of Nigeria, Pakistan, Bangladesh, Egypt, Indonesia, Iran, Mexico, the Philippines, Turkey, South Korea and Vietnam. Both Iran and Pakistan appear to be posed the best for being the next formal BRICS members. Turkey obviously, has recently back-fired on the unipolar NATO alliance in their Syrian shenanigans, having flat-out shot themselves in the foot and now leaving this group to be dubbed the "N-10". Following Russia's exposing to the world, Turkey's illegal oil sales by its president the Turkish president then followed orders from the Zionist-controlled U.S. and EU coalition, to shoot down a Russian fighter jet. These barbarous acts have cost Turkey dearly pushing it out of the orbit of necessary trade relations while decoupling it into a new isolation and destitution, at a time when it was on the cusp of inheriting its greatest opportunities, such as the South Stream gas pipeline with Russia. Turkey's people came ever-so-close to "having it all" as it would have controlled 75% of Europe's heating fuel. They are now stuck only raped and robbed by a president who should be "shot at dawn" for the extent of corruption, malpractice, murder and mayhem he is guilty of.

The "Next Ten" then, along with the BRICS nations are among the world's largest economies of the 21st century. They possess the best investment outlook for future growth. Judging from a strategic standpoint with Turkey's recent expulsion from this group in terms of demand, appeal and the lack of future associations, it will only raise the pressure on the N-10 to fast-track their future BRICS' membership. Turkey's macroeconomic stability, political maturity and trade opportunities, have all been destroyed by one gluttonous president while his actions have now branded NATO globally, as a very reckless criminal alliance which no longer adheres to international law, or treaties and is an accomplice to State-sponsored terrorism. The Turkish peoples' only remaining hope for rescuing their hard-earned "once-in-a-lifetime opportunities", would be in ousting their President Erdogan, arrest terrorists and repair its ties with Russia. Need I remind all neutral observers that Erdogan committed to a much greater extent, the identical crimes to which the West had Saddam Hussein hung and executed for. This in and of itself now broadcasts globally that the elite Jewish terrorist-controlled West has even become notorious for flip-flopping in matters of illicit business and foreign policy delinquencies, outside its accumulating high crimes of international law, treaties and human rights violations!

The West's Zionist media may package it in whatever ways it chooses, but the fact yet remains evident that Qatar, Saudi Arabia, Israel, the U.S. and EU are now vividly imprinted in the fronts of all nations' minds worldwide, as being supporters of State-sponsored terrorism.

This new change in the geopolitical shuffle bodes extremely dire consequences to all countries within the outdated, dinosaur structure known as NATO. No disrespect to President Buhari for diverting our attention from him for a moment, but in order to fully understand Nigeria's situation in the world it becomes necessary to realize the current changes underway within the global environment to which Nigeria must now contend with and operate under. Globally speaking "the rules have now forever changed". A time has arrived which no one can stop that says the U.S., EU, Israel and Saudi Arabia have become too outdated, overspent, corrupt and out-of-sync with the new global tides, to further qualify themselves with any global economic leadership. Their global standing has expired as they dwindle into the halls of history as "yesterday's leadership". The greatest thing they can do for their people now is to accept and find closure in it all "peacefully", pass the batons to Russia, China and Brazil, etc. and see how best they can fit into becoming a benefactor of this new global landscape as a team player and collaborative partner.

As things currently stand, the member nations of NATO are performing an extremely dangerous act by remaining rutted in an outdated line of thinking. It is as if they are obeying in unison, one screaming Rockefeller child who's only words are, "No, I don't want to share"! Leadership within the NATO nations has become grossly antiquated and delusional. They live deathly in fear of having to become team players in a league where they can no longer always have things their way, or dominate the relationship. Their biased indifference is sentencing their citizenry to a future of poverty and bleakness in a ridiculous and completely unnecessary temper tantrum of destabilization and destruction. My only advice to them: drop all Russia - Iran sanctions, stop supporting terrorism and leave NATO or die. Die in a nuclear Armageddon!

As for Nigeria's President Muhammadu Buhari, here are a few things he might consider to help his country best get back on track:

- **Streamline the bureaucracy**: Nigeria has more than 500 State owned corporations and agencies, many of which could be merged or sold-off or dismantled. In the past, these have only served inside politicians by appointments or as crony capitalist deals among insiders, both elements which need a good shaking-out anyways. They also are fertile beds for corruption. Millions could be raised immediately from this urgently needed overhaul alone.

- **Change your nickname**: (It currently is "Baba go slow") From "Baba go slow and steady" to "The Intelligent Jaguar" or something. Time is very much of the essence these days, demanding smart yet swift executions of working policies that can be put into action.

According to a report from the African Development Bank Nigeria's 36 States needed to have their budgetary trends consolidated, trimmed or under review. The Buhari administration has been forced to bailout 27 State budgets which altogether total some $2.1 billion. State governors need to get their own financial houses in order, even if this means making cuts and raising certain taxes.

Each State needs to reexamine their economic potentials through innovation and broadening their views of their own future, beyond oil and metals. They mustn't play China's approaching investments as "just another handout" as it is a nation who's well-seasoned at spotting all the leaks to development. President Buhari knows better than anyone that reckless, misguided State spending breeds military coups.

- **Enforce your anti-corruption campaigns very carefully**: Though the All progressive Congress (APC) and its party have their share of kleptomaniacs, better to silently neutralize only the most steadfast of the bunch, than to risk stampeding the whole herd against you. The U.S. Justice Department once accused an APC governor of stealing more than $450 million from their State's coffers for former dictator Sani Abacha.

"Cleaning house" can be akin to walking through a minefield for a well-intended president. This predicament requires discretion in carefully choosing your prosecutions in a most wise fashion. One that will enable you to achieve the greater good, but without committing political suicide in the process.

- **<u>Don't waste revenues</u>**: Especially on wholly owned State companies, or the industries of "yesterdays" oil and mining production. Instead, modernize with deliberate policies, attract investments for innovative and entrepreneurial new industries and treat yourself to at least one visit to speak with Vladimir Putin. Both he and Russia (as well as President Xi of China) can offer invaluable insight to these, as they've already tested 100's of models. Learn from your BRICS cousins what the demands for the future will be and stimulate and promote good small business sense and practices.

- **<u>Make smart, historic policy and govern with a consciousness</u>**: And one that will outlive yourself. You are a unique man, so your memories can linger on in the wisdom of what legislation you make today. This may at times require uncomfortable partnerships but putting into place smart, historic and innovative legislation may perpetuate not only your legacy but your people's prosperity as well.

For example, changing (or even abolishing) Nigeria's "security votes". These are perceived by many outside critics to be just budgetary line items which are nothing more than wasteful "slush funds" and represent funds that could be put to better use stimulating economic growth through small business incentives and attracting new start-ups.

In September of 2015, President Muhammadu Buhari addressed the United Nations General Assembly on Climate Change. His speech was decent, yet short and is as follows:

"Excellencys, heads of State and government, Secretary General of the United Nations, President of the 70$^{th}$ UNGA (United Nations General Assembly), distinguished delegates, ladies and gentleman,"

"This summit provides a unique opportunity for us to work together to address climate change and its impacts which is an undeniable issue to the international community. The increase in global warming is an indication that we face a crisis of global proportions".

"Excellencys, the world is experiencing new and unusual climate variability due to increased emissions of greenhouse gases. Even though Africa contributes very little to global warming, the socio-economic consequences of climate change spare no nation. The burden is just as overwhelming for developing countries".

"In Nigeria we have seen extreme weather variations, rising sea levels, encroaching desertification, excessive rainfall, erosion and floods; land degradation, all of which threaten the ecosystem. These developments have devastating human costs and are affecting food security, livelihoods and the very survival of our people. To address these negative affects we have developed a national policy to guide Nigeria's response to climate change. Our response is broadly based on the twin strategy of mitigation and adaptation".

"As a party to the climate change convention and its protocol, Nigeria is strongly committed to the adoption of a legally binding, universal agreement to mitigate climate change. We commend countries that have announced their Intended Nationally Determined Contributions (INDC) ahead of the October, 2015 deadline. These contributions will go a long way in reducing the greenhouse gas emissions worldwide. The INDC will serve as a yardstick for measuring the commitment of parties to the Framework Convention".

“In addition, we must prioritize the means of implementing the INDC, in terms of finance, technology and capacity-building, especially in supporting developing countries, including those in Africa. This is fundamental in ensuring that the collective action to combat climate change is indeed collaborative and effective in the long run”.

As we approach Paris, the Nigerian position which reflects the African consensus is that a legally binding, universal instrument will be beneficial to all State parties. Nigeria will continue to champion the core principles and goals of the new sustainable development agenda and hopes that the next conference of parties will eventually become a global milestone to combat and cushion the impacts of climate change. The Paris agreement should be rules-based, predictable and robust to adequately address climate change vulnerabilities. It is essential that the least developing countries and small island States receive the institutional capacity support for mitigation, adaptation, gender and climate change linkages towards building a sustainable environment”.

“Collective action remains the only viable option to addressing the challenges of global warming and the ever-growing impact of climate change”.

“Excellencys, we have no other choice, but to protect our environment for the benefit of the present and the future generations. Collectively we have to work towards achieving this all important objective. I thank you"!

# Chapter VIII

## Law Enforcement or Armageddon

Probably one of the most interesting things I have learned from the studies of multipolar and unipolar models are twofold. One, "coexistence" vs "domination" and two, "free-thinking" vs "brain-washed mind-control". Though we who have awakened in the West have our hearts and minds in the multipolar consciousness, the remnants of unipolarity still litters our universe.

If what remains of the unipolar existence cannot soon "coexist" with us, it might very well attempt to destroy us all, including itself.

The unipolar masters are another tale entirely, but as for the people who make-up its world, its citizens, they must come to realize and accept that they are trapped in a catch-22. If they do not rebel and win against their masters, they will be sentenced to a life of demoralizing subservience. A subservience that will end in Armageddon, since its masters would be out of control of the peoples' consensus, while the masters themselves are already out of control.

And if the unipolar world's citizens rise up and succeed in gaining control of their masters, living with the amount of damage and devastation they have already imposed upon its people economically, in emaciation of their sovereignty and liberties, their ethics and the erosion of their moral fiber socially (destruction of families), will prove to be a form of sentencing too, but at least one gets to live to see their victory's spoils slowly implemented. That initial acceptance however, would entail that all former unipolar citizens must start at the bottom of the development ladder once again. It will require "three generations" to repair the devastation and destruction its former masters have laid in their wake. It would mean that the majority of Europeans and Americans would have to adjust to living as Third World citizens for almost the same duration, In order to adjust, three generations might very well have to accept all sharing the same households and if they were lucky enough to secure employment the pay scales and conditions might resemble those found in places like Zimbabwe, Burundi, Haiti, Sudan, Uganda, Myanmar and the Philippines, as they were some 70 years ago. It would be a throwback existence, a complete reset of the unipolar world that requires "starting all over again". Yes it would demand Europeans and Americans making sweat-shop products to export to China, Russia, Brazil and even Mexico and the Japanese would be included in this scenario as well.

Armageddon or successful control of our former unipolar masters. These are the only two options remaining in the West's deck of cards, if it does not come to its senses very, very soon!

Islamic countries play a very vital and crucial role in the global financial interlock of the BRICS multipolarity. Pakistan, Nigeria, Egypt and Iran are among the leading contenders for entering the BRICS polarity. Turkey's president has as was already mentioned, forced his peoples' nation out of the loop. President Vladimir Putin's Russia assumed the presidency of the BRICS during January of 2015. Brazil, Russia, China, South Africa and their constituent members all hold great promise, though at this writing it looking as though Brazil might have just fallen into the clutches of the CIA and Western neocons once again. India, once based as a BRICS centerpiece is now in a similar process of what occurred in Turkey, only their prime minister and president are using the "pair of smiling Jacks" approach. Covertly they are attempting an "infiltration" by incorporating their own methods of corruption, while they increasingly aid the BRICS arch enemies.

This is all being orchestrated independently and in opposition to India's people; to play the instrument of one while using the sheet music from another. Prime Minister Modi and President Mukherjee are being counted on by the unipolar masters to successfully aid them in performing a 9-11 attack to the BRICS' structural architecture, leaving India's citizens in the middle to fend for themselves. It is for this that Indian leadership remains a very dangerous element to the multipolar structure by utilizing its superficial, collaborative means to play both sides of the fence.

Authentic BRICS countries share a goal to change the existing world order at all levels, from vital security issues to the global financial instruments and economic systems. They view the hegemony of one country and its allies as misguided and dangerous, hence they favor a multipolar approach and assembly, thereby leveling the playing field by granting all players equality. With much thanks to Moscow's and Beijing's leadership, the BRICS approach is aimed at the harmonization of interests for all with cohesive collaborations seeking win-win results as President Xi had mentioned in his historic speech.

More and more experts are reporting that without the participation of the Islamic countries, both the cultural and civil meld of the BRICS architectural anatomy would not have been possible. Islamic countries are proving to be major I-beams of support to the multipolar structure, especially in terms of Islamic banking which is now on the cusp of having a much wider presence into the mainstream. An ever-growing portion of the Western citizenry is beginning to realize that it is "organized Zionist Jewry" which seeks to sabotage the Muslim culture and not actual extremists forged by their own making.

"It is due to this intelligent awakening that countries such as Indonesia, the world's largest Muslim country in terms of population, are quickly ascending as the next candidates to be absorbed into the BRICS coalition. The construction of the "Southern Transport Corridor" is living proof that the trade turnovers of Islamic countries such as Pakistan, Egypt, Iran and Indonesia are growing more rapidly. New directions into political and financial spheres can be realized for Islamic countries with the BRICS acting as their consolidating association. Countries such as Iran can now actively participate in the newly established Development Bank.

The increasing multiple numbers of countries unhappy with the unilateral hegemony of Israel's United States colony, is proving to only increase the velocity of the new BRICS memberships. America as an Israeli colony with WASP front men lobbying, campaigning and screaming for "more, more war" and "hate, hate, bait" serves only the 1%, Zionist elitists; an already proven model of complete failure and exclusiveness. So it's not by chance that the BRICS win-win and all-inclusive approach is gaining in popularity among the world's many promising nations. The citizens of the West are tired of being lied to and misrepresented, just as Islamic nations have had enough of being propagandized and falsely portrayed.

Multilateral cooperation must replace the American policy and afford the Islamic world a practical integration of mutual respect, dignity and constructive collaboration and not of the divisive, domineering hate and deceit it currently practices! The assimilation of Islamic countries into a more peace-loving, multilateral composition more fully benefits all involved. This association of States will become the embodiment of a new concept, one born of international relations with a more equitable distribution of global governance, based on East - West, and South partnerships.

This will in turn lead to a humanitarian dialogue globally, whereas in comparison the unilateral agenda offers none of these above vital elements. Once Venezuela, Argentina, Bolivia, Mongolia and Malaysia become fully absorbed into the BRICS sphere, its profile will surpass that of the United States and Europe combined, resulting in about 1.3 of the world's economic output and 50% of its global inhabitants. Over the past few years Asia alone registered an 8% average growth rate, in comparison to the West's 0 to 1%.

The key to the BRICS success is to solidify their union with solidarity, facilitate common trade policies and decouple their economies from the U.S. dollar. While the West, in its adamant and pigheaded refusal to accept equality over domination, has accidently had its mask slip off. What the world sees is an identical reenactment by the same Zionist instigators leading up to WW II in Germany and to the Bolshevik Revolution of Russia. The world is not as naive as Zionist media portrays it. BRICS countries are concerned of the West's many former optimists now describing the futility of Western people's predicament. Paul Craig Roberts, Dr. Lasha Darkmoon and scores of others who were seen as the West's last remaining seekers of hope in constructive peace, are now currently describing it as being a foregone conclusion.

They now interpret the West to no longer be a democracy, but rather a crypto-fascist State with a culture that, as in old Germany and Bolshevik Russia, the Zionists have succeeded in causing it to have fermented into a quagmire of neo-paganist nihilism. This is usually the precursor to a major war and a loss in life of extreme proportions. Combining WW II and the Bolshevik Revolution alone, we're talking somewhere in the neighborhood of between 100 million to 140 million people dead.

Therefore, in order for this book to carry any viable portrayal of a realistic substance I must face this issue straight on. So what does one call this place, this moment in time all of us in world have come to? I can only best describe it as humanity's great fork in the road. The one fork leads to an acceptance to the West's current State of existence which we all know with the Zionists now having their fingers on its nuclear triggers means death to us all. Down the alternate fork, survival and a great awakening that breathes new life into "hope" where others have surrendered it.

I must address this issue, due plainly to the fact that it not only means for the continuation of the BRICS ascension, but the very survival to all of humanity. "Zionism" or criminal-Jewry must first be acknowledged and realized by the masses for what it is; a killer virus, a pandemic, or a mega-plague. All people should respect all cultures and faiths (except Satanism), including Jews. To discuss 1-to-2% of the Jewish element the Zionist criminals, in a complete separation from the remaining 98-to-99% is respectfully objective and not anti-Semitic.

If the world is to avert total devastation of the human species by addressing the cause it must do so in the same fashion as an organic chemist who searches a cure to disease for a Big Pharma pharmaceutical company, or as any chemist might search for a remedy application for a large corporation who develops pesticides. We first must "isolate the pest" or host from all else. In order to rise above the atrocious and holocaustic methods of the past, where a wicked campaign was waged to kill all related bloodlines to the cause demands diligent focus. When an orchard experiences an infestation of fruit flies, killing every fly in existence is the ignorance of a lost focus.

Americans can lend "support to Israel's citizenry" without giving one dime to its government. If any organization operating in the West is found to be using funds that support the virus in question, namely the Zionist criminal element, it should be treated as a crime syndication. Most all of Zionist criminality in the America can be completely eradicated with just the enforcement of one law that's been on the books since 1970. "The Rico Act" or the Racketeer Influenced and Corrupt Organizations Act. No U.S. president in 52 years has ever attempted to treat the Zionist virus in question as a crime syndicate, or invading force. Once the people demand it, if enforced it would cause the seizure and liquidation of Goldman Sachs, all the major television media companies in the

U.S., quite a few major Jewish fund-raising organizations and several major brokerage houses on Wall Street just for openers.

It is the Western people's choice. Have their laws enforced against the 1% killer virus or have it destroy us all in one last nuclear war. World peace is the second application that would make the Zionist Crime Syndicate collapse. In order to survive it needs conflicts and wars with an economic base of weapons production and causing destruction. Until its last gasping breath it seeks to forever divide; that's how this virus spreads.

Ten years ago 90% of the world's reserves were denominated in U.S. currency. As of this writing that number has dropped to nearly 50%. Soon a tectonic shift of the geopolitical plates not seen since 1683 when the Ottoman Empire failed at the gates of Vienna, will quake. And when they do the West's 1% will only be finding their names handsomely embossed on the faces of public toilets.

# Chapter IX

## West's Slumbering Mole

India's President Pranab Mukherjee seems to think very highly of himself at his own website, but this controversial slippery jackal seems to have an uncanny talent for avoiding accountability as one of India's leading high-profile politicians. During the Indian Congress' monopoly of power Mukherjee held some important positions. The scale of corruption during those years was so high, it reached uncontrollable levels with no oversight or investigations ever being formally launched. With a dismissive attitude followed by mud-slinging fests, is how each scandal or allegation was met.

Known to some as "the clever puffer fish", he created an extremely dense smoke screen and the public was never allowed to hang around once the smoke had cleared. Lord Acton was once quoted as saying, "Power tends to corrupt and absolute power corrupts absolutely". Panchayat minister Subrata Mukherjee said, "Pranab owes a lot to India's Marist and Left Front". And "this" is the very keystone to the riddle of India today, for it is the paramount clue as to my final prognosis that India is "a genuine wolf in sheep's clothing" and is heavily disguised to be a BRICS player when in actuality it is "unipolar" at the very heart of its leadership! Both Russia and China must become increasingly aware of this fact, for it will prove to be the complete destruction of the BRICS from the inside out, if it is not monitored like a hawk! Subrata went onto to say, "When Pranab first started his career in the Bengal Congress, he then also received a lot of help from the Marxists".

On the surface his controversies always seem to arise from his suspicious nature. Wikileaks documents obtained in 2011 confirmed the U.S. had their doubts about Murherjee as Finance Minister. The Times of India featured this in a cable to the U.S. Embassy in Delhi of September, 2009, where a U.S. Secretary of State asked, "To which business groups is Murherjee beholden"? Why was he chosen over Montek? To which industrial or business groups is Pranab Mukherjee beholden? Whom will he seek to help through his policies? What are Mukherjee's priorities in the upcoming budget"?

His continuing claims to fame is he not only holds the record for putting the highest percentage of India's Parliament to sleep when he speaks, but he has also been photographed several times being asleep on the job himself. It would appear that "the magic of the Marxists" seem to make many things disappear for this man. I say this because all the allegations against him never get investigated. The group "India Against Corruption" still would like Mr. Mukherjee's ties to the following exposed:

- The Navy War Room Leak case

- The Rice Scam

- The Scorpene Submarine case

He is also mentioned in an Export Scam.

Nonetheless, President Pranab Mukherjee can best be dismissed as a master "body blocker". His background shows a history of serving as a diversional front man while each time the big sharks of his affiliations can ransack backstage, uninterrupted and undetected. His questionable integrity, lack transparency and escapes from accountability says blatantly, he is in no way an authentic multipolar leader. A much more fitting profile would be as a "Western unipolar mole". A slumbering mole who lines his pockets well in return for leaving the gate to the corral open, seems well afoot here. Western Zionist merry pranksters and the whole NWO destabilization crew are quietly being put into position now, as New Delhi burns. With India's economy and agriculture fully hijacked, Western-Israeli shenanigans are soon to follow along the India-Pakistan and China borders.

Having a complete lack of statesmanship, fairness, or regard for protocol and justice, he and his prior minister were directly involved with the notorious Hasan Ali of Pune who, while being investigated for $8.6 billion in one of his Swiss bank accounts. The case was eventually dropped after Mr. Mukherjee joyfully announced with a smirk, that all the money had disappeared from Hasan Ali's account, whose balance mysteriously dropped to only $50,000. The president is still under popular suspicion of aiding and abetting banking schemes and white collar criminals who are hiding large sums of money fleeced from the Government of India, in overseas bank accounts. He has even been accused of intentionally road-blocking investigations while making no attempts to retrieve these funds. All this goes on while his Marxist cohorts periodically sanitize Google, to wipe any negativity from the West's internet.

Whether or not Mr. Mukherjee's congressionally controlled media will succeed in denying the public the true nature of this man through his entire presidency, remains to be seen. In a deliberate display to avoid any controversial allegations against him, his website yet remains a testament to his repackaged image. But for those who look for it the truths are visible under the layers of make-up.

Another of this puffer fish's magnificent and profitable schemes were in milking his publicity bandwagon as free advertising for the sale of his election campaign's propagandized autobiography release. Yet even this has proven not to be immune to his infamous, dismissive disposition as it was finely crafted to side-step the needed details of the scandals that have plagued his government reign.

Good leaderships have a natural ability of attracting the attention of their colleagues, as well as the public's. But as history has proven (with live video), few can remain awake through an entire speech made by a well-known thief professing to represent your best interests. With television footage showing half of his colleagues fast asleep, the soporific effects of his speeches are a clearer sign of mundane double-speak. It would appear these extended effects have now reached the rest of India where all are asleep.

With a popular picture still floating around Facebook showing Mukherjee soundly asleep himself at his former job, he has been anointed by India Today as being one of Parliament's former

“Sleeping Beauties”. In the real world outside, while his homeland slumbers through the silent Modi-Mukherjee rape and pillage of a once great nation, any national or international professionals falling asleep at their posts are promptly terminated. This president’s power seems to ever elude justice, as the sleeping mole will prove to be a different form of back-stab to the BRICS, than Erdogan’s was to NATO. A systemic virus who silently and slowly attacks from within, he is no less dangerous than a Russian fighter pilot getting shot in the back.

Deceit and corruption once surrounded the troubled “Emergency” once imposed by then Prime Minister Indira Ghandi (1975 – 1977). Having been responsible for many of the excesses of that time, Pranab Mukherjee was summoned by the Sha Commission. Mukherjee and Gandhi both subsequently refused to step down. The Indian Express wrote:” The commission was a fact-finding commission. On the basis of its report, the government could have taken action. But nothing was done,” said a former commission member, now a police officer. “The only people who faced a tough time due to the inquiry report, were those people who were part of the commission”.

Former member of the Central Board of Direct Taxes, V.U. Eradi, is the officer who dealt with the tax matters of the Shah Commission. In 2011 he wrote a powerful article, “Put in the Dock by the Shah Commission” he wrote: “Based on the above it would not be unreasonable to ask the Finance Minister to specify, in which case where a ton of primary gold with Swiss markings was discovered, was he put in the dock by the Shah Commission. History and propriety demand an honest answer”. That’s rightly well put, but as time and Mr. Mukherjee’s ways would have it, any meaningful response remains negligible, in all probability.

In India, other papers have also surfaced. K.N. Arun wrote: “Pranab has the dubious distinction of being one of the ministers to be indicted by the Shah Commission, set up by the Janata

Parliament government to go into the Emergency excesses. Among the charges in which he was indicted, related to the illegal arrest and jailing of Gayatri Devi and Colonel Bhawani Singh, Maharani and Maharaja of Jaipur. Gayatri Devi, a leading light of the Swantatra Party, had been a member of Parliament. In its report submitted in 1978, the Shah Commission observed that Mukherjee had misused his position and abused his authority in ordering the detention of Smt. Gayatri Devi and Col. Bhawani Singh. It is clearly a case of subversion of lawful process and of administration procedures".

Mukherjee was also indicted on charges of falsifying the files relating to Gayatri Devis's arrest. Arun further comments, "In fact, the L.P. Singh Committee, set up by the Morarji Desai government to take follow-up action on the Shah Commission findings, had ordered a police investigation into the criminal falsification of the file relating to Gayatri Devi's arrest, as well as Pranab's role in the jailing of Jaipur's Maharaja and Maharani". Though the police report was filed, it was withdrawn upon Mrs. Gandhi's return to power. It is fairly well demonstrated here, a pattern of non-accountability. There would be no objection to purposely conceal evidence if the individuals had nothing to hide.

India's president has further criminality in his background of possible extortion, taking bribes and racketeering surrounding Mukherjee's role with Reliance Industries. In the article, "Pranab pressured by Sebi to go easy on RIL", shows evidence documented in stating, "a month and a half before he demitted office, former Sebi member K.M. Abraham wrote an anguished letter to the Prime Minister alleging pressure from Finance Minister Pranab Mukherjee and his advisor Omita Paul, to 'manage' cases against powerful corporate groups who were being investigated by Sebi. But another case involving insider trading by Reliance Industries Ltd. Is still to be decided. And in this case Abraham clearly alleges that Sebi Chairman U.K, Sinha had been pressuring him to find a way to get the Mukesh Ambani Company off the hook. If Abraham had his way, Reliance would have been fined in the consent order: There has been no independent investigation into this matter".

Had Pranab Mukherjee been a Chinese Finance Minister under China's President Xi Jinping, he would have been immediately sacked, fined and sent to prison indefinitely. Mukherjee later came to the aid of an unlikely Bengali Bollywood Damsel in Distress (Pranab being himself Bengaline), Ms. Taslima Nasreen, a foul mouthed heroine. Islamist groups had forewarned Ms. Nasreen on numerous occasions of being offended by her writings. The Bengal Government threw her out in 2007 and she came under the auspices of Mr. Mukherjee's Central Government. To the astonishment of her critics, as well as the Bengal Islamic community, Mr. Mukherjee awarded her full protection under Federal Security officials at an undisclosed location. It was a blatant demonstration of discriminatory treatment and favoritism, as Mukherjee afforded Taslima Nasreen the complete opposite of what Salman Rushdie had received.

The Times of India wrote, "It was a strange experience in Kokata, Nasreen was free to roam, write and chatter. Here even the next door neighbors had no clue she was living among them. She soon began to chaff under all the restrictions. Even the cook in the safehouse was not quite it. He couldn't cook fish (Ms. Nasreen's main diet). Pranab Mukherjee's household arranged for the fish from Chittaranjar Park, plus a cook sources said. Then by the end of January she fell sick and had to be kept under observation at AIIMS. They wanted Taslima to keep quiet and out of the headlines for a few months, until the dust had settled and then she could return to Kolkata. But she had become, according to sources, very querulous at this time asking for all kinds of things".

It has been said by many since, both by critics and associates alike that this incident reflected a new degree of decadence for Mukherjee. While wasting valuable public funds by caving into the demands of his Bengal diva, he seemed to give no considerations to India's 360 million living in poverty, that one Indian farmer was dying every 30 minutes, or that 50% of child deaths are caused by malnutrition. As all the skeletons in President Pranab Mukherjees come home to roost, many shutter at the thought that such a man is now in charge of prioritizing resources to ensure India's most vulnerable.

Renowned senior politician and eminent lawyer Ram Jethmalani wrote a powerful, no-holes-barred piece in the Sunday Guardian.com's "Ethics and Power" section titled, "Open Letter to Pranab". Mr. Jethmalani's article reads as follows:

"This letter is being signed by a few like-minded citizens who know something about your political history and what part you have played in Indian politics so far. The signatories believe that what they write is the opinion of the overwhelming majority of the people of India...,"

"Limitations of space and time both necessarily compel me to render only a truthful and accurate summary of the people's case against you. The present epistle is in the form of a charge sheet, presented in the court of the Sovereign people of India, who will themselves speak after two years"….,

**Charge #1:** During the scandalous Emergency imposed by Indira Ghandi in 1975 and the resulting suspension of human rights of all citizens and the virtual demise of democracy, you were a very loyal, though small time supporter of the Emergency. You fully supported and participated in its misdeeds. You cannot honestly claim, that at least in some small measure, you expressed your disapproval of its evil, or that you prevented a single atrocity inflicted upon some honest citizens. Citizens possessed of the highest intellectual, moral and spiritual qualifications were victims. You saved none. Throughout the Emergency you acted like a loyal servant of the Gandhi family and what is worse, you were a complete collaborator with the main criminal of the Emergency, the late Sanjay Gandhi. You treated him as your boss".

"Recently some time in 2010 you wrote a book on the 125th anniversary of the Congress Party. In this book you openly indicted Sanjay Gandhi being solely responsible for all the excesses of the government during this disgraceful period of 1975 – 1977. This statement of yours is a true and voluntary confession. You have pleaded guilty to the charge that the Emergency was an unconstitutional aberration, but you suggest that the person responsible was Sanjay Gandhi. You are trying to find a post humus defense for his mother. What kind of a Prime Minister was she to have achieved her duty to the nation and allowed an uneducated automobile repairman son to lodge innocent people in jail and lunatic wards, to suppress the freedom of the press and cover-up all his crimes with the slogan, "India is Indira and Indira is India""? You are the originator of this slogan and we believe that Devkant Barua learned it from you and not the other way around. During this period you were a Minister of State for Revenue and Expenditure. You have not been able to claim not even today, that you gave any good advice for Sanjay and that he desisted because of your advice".

**Charge #2:** You were a party to the inhumane and wholly illegal incarceration of two of India's great women, the late Gayatyri Devi and the Rajata Vijaya Rajie of Gwalior, both cultivated and socially evolved souls in the cells of prisons, condemned to death in Tihar jail".

"From one of them you have even recorded a note that she should be released, but under pressure, you super-imposed on it anew note with a wholly opposite opinion. The Shah Commission recording a finding that you committed a forgery and destroyed evidence of your own opinion on that rare occasion".

"Your services rendered to Sanjay and his mother were obviously appreciated by the two major criminals. After the ignominious fall of the Janata government, you were duly rewarded for your Emergency services with a promotion as the full-fledged Minister of Finance. This reward was obviously also for another great service which you rendered to both of them, before the fall of the Janata government. This consists of your conduct before the Shah Commission. The following finding of the Shah Commission is worth quoting. 'Pranab Mukherjee assisted the Commission at the preliminary stage of the fact finding inquiry, he didn't file any statement in the case, as was required to be done under Rule 5 (2) (a) of the Commission Inquiry Act, 1952. But he refused to take oath and render evidence'.

"Your confessions of 2010 shows your knowledge of the Shah Commission and helped it to determine the truth? Of course you did show your loyalty to your erstwhile benefactors and conspirators, but you failed in your duty to the truth and democracy. The Emergency was over and nobody had any fear from the new government. Even then, you did not summon courage to speak the truth".

**Charge #3:** "That thereafter you had been a member of every Cabinet in a Congress, or Congress-led government. In the 1980's, as Commerce and Finance Minister, you were better known for tailoring policies to favor a particular corporate group, to the extent that both in Parliament and in the press you were dubbed as a minister for that corporate group. Your ideological orientation towards crony capitalism has further been exposed in your present stint as Finance Minister, by a former SEBI board member, K.M. Abraham, who has accused you and your powerful officer on special duty of being aligned with certain corporate groups, including your long time favorites. You have always been associated with the Rice Export scam, nor did you distinguish yourself for integrity as Minister for Defense between 2004 and 2006 during which tenure, both the Scorpen deal and the Navy War Room Leak cases surfaced".

**Charge #4:** "One of the signatories to this letter is Mr. Ram Jethmalani. In an article published by him around the year 2000 on "The Role of the President under the Constitution of India", he writes: 'Whatever be the President's legal powers, his real power rests on his moral stature and the public esteem he enjoys. With a nod of disapproval, or a twinkle in his eye, A President can bring back to the straight track of probity and wisdom, a derailed Council of Ministers. A threat from the President to resign and take the people into confidence, when he is asked to act against the law, Constitution, or Salus Populi, can make a Prime Minister retrace his steps. Unfortunately, at least one President disgraced the office, by declaring a phony Emergency. The President must act as a conscience of a nation and political parties should resist the temptation of looking for rubber stamps".

"We don't think any sensible person would disagree about this supreme qualification of a President. We charge that you do not possess this qualification in any shape or form. You are totally bereft of it, with your accompanying August being a disgrace to the

Republic of India. Bengal has given us stalwarts like Bankim Chandra Chatterjee, Swami Vive Kanada, Deshbandu Chitteranjan Das, Sri Huro Bindo, Rash Behari Bose, Rabindrahath Tagore and many others. You are a disgrace to each of them".

..., Mr. Ram Jethmalani had listed 9 charges, which can be accessed online. It has become clearly evident that Pranab Mukherjee is a walking cancer to the multipolar BRICS and to any office he holds. In his entire career he has proven to be nothing more than a Teflon political criminal and the West's slumbering mole.

# Chapter X

## The West's Tavistock Brainwash

Some 23 years ago Dr. John Coleman, a former MI6 agent, wrote a book in stunning detail called, "Conspirators' Hierarchy: The Story of the Committee of 300". In specific reference to his pioneering investigations into the "Tavistock Institute's" backgrounds and projects, the school's main figures sought to learn and synthesize the works of such varied thinkers as Kant, Hegel,

Marx, Freud, Weber and Luckacs. Tavistock was a follow-up of the Frankfort School, a predominantly Jewish group of philosophers and Marxist theorists who fled Germany after Hitler shutdown their "Institute for Social Research" at the University of Frankfort.

Dr. Coleman often complained that New World Order expose' writers were often guilty of using his research without crediting him. In 2001 a Dr. Byron T. Weeks sent a highly detailed letter to one John Quinn of "NewsHawk Inc.".

The letter of Byron T. Weeks, MD, Col. USAF, MC, Ret, is as follows:

"Formed in 1947, the Tavistock Institute is an independent, not-for-profit organization which seeks to combine research in the social sciences with professional practice. Problems of the institution-building and organizational design and change are being tackled in all sectors of government, industry and commerce, health and welfare, education, etc. – nationally and internationally and clients range from multinationals to small community groups. A growth area has been the use of a developmental approach to evaluation of new and experimental programs, particularly in health, education and community development. This has also produced new training events alongside the regular program of group relations conferences. The institute owns and edits the monthly journal, 'Human Relations' (published by Plenum Press), which is now in its 48$^{th}$ year and has recently launched (in conjunction with Sage Publications) a new journal 'Evaluation".

"Three elements combine to make the Institute unusual, if not unique. It has the independence of being entirely self-financing with no subsidies from government or other sources. The action research orientation places it between but not in, the worlds of academia and consultancy. Its range of disciplines include anthropology, economics, organizational behavior, political science, psychoanalysis, psychology and sociology".

"The ideology of 'American Foundations' was created by Tavistock Institute of Human Relations in London. In 1921 the Duke of Beford, Marquess of Tavistock, and the 11th Duke gave a building to the Institute to study the effect of shellshock on British soldiers who survived World War I. Its purpose was to establish the 'breaking point' of men under stress, under the direction of the British Army Bureau of Psychological Warfare, commanded by Sir John Rawlings – Reese".

---

- *<u>**Author's special note**</u> <u>(JP Cassone')</u>: Of all the people to make one their prophet, Freud was probably one of "investigative history's" worst. He was a verified, severe cocaine addict and had an extremely negative view of women. Most of his many demented theories have since been successfully discredited today. He obviously suffered from some strange sexual experiences as a child, perhaps sexually abused and he persistently hid these experiences, but chose to manifest them into his theories, as he often broad-brushed all of humanity to be the same as himself. In addition, one has to ask what kind of psychologist would chain-smoke 35 cigars-a-day, be diagnosed with cancer and yet always personally fail to attain the will to quit smoking, which would eventually take his life?

In the end, Sigmund Freud appears to be quite the imposter who was not the originator of psychoanalysis, the relationship of the subconscious, nor the interpretation of dreams. He was only the first individual to make them popular and to profit from them. He was a grossly demented and psychologically damaged and crippled individual with a severe nicotine-cocaine addiction who successfully hoodwinked an aristocracy that likely shared many of his same addictions and psychotic afflictions! And it is from individuals like these which the New World Order has used as its mortar to its original foundational blocks. Their very neurotic methods, policies and proclamations have pollinated a heightened sense of delusion so extreme in fact, that far-flung ambitions such as "how to break the will of 99% of all humanity" and "how to destroy its families, freedoms, identity, as well as its countries' sovereignty and governments" have all been instigated and originally hatched by this criminally elite's insanity! As you will learn, many historically prominent individuals such as Churchill, Roosevelt and the many others which followed them whom you might have once held in high esteem, will shell-shock most readers once they are revealed more about the make-up of their true conduct, practices and actual aspirations! It further substantiates that the very first undermining attempts which conspired to overthrow the West's democracies, originated "at the top", from their select few affluent families and from within the offices of their very own Heads of State! * -

---

"Tavistock Institute is headquartered in London. Its prophet Sigmund Freud, settled in Marshfield Gardens when he moved to England. Freud was given a mansion by Princess Bonaparte. Tavistock's pioneer work in behavioral science along Freudian lines of 'controlling' humans, established it as the world center of foundational ideology. Its network now extends from the University of Sussex to the U.S. through the Stanford Research Institute, Esalen, MIT, Hudson Institute, Heritage Foundation, Center of Strategic and International Studies at Georgetown, where State Department, U.S. Airforce Intelligence and the Rand and Mitre corporations' personnel are trained. They are all required to undergo indoctrination at one or more of their Tavistock controlled institutions. A network of secret groups, the Mont Perelin Society, Trilaterial Commission, Ditchley Foundation and the Club of Rome serve as conduit for instructions to the Tavistock network".

"Tavistock Institute developed the mass brain-washing techniques which were first experimented upon American prisoners of war in Korea.

---

- *<u>**Author's special note**</u> <u>(JP Cassone')</u>: This also shows a covert, corporate collusion with the enemy's side in a major war and it further demonstrates how most wars are falsely orchestrated for the sole benefit of bankers and corporate researchers.

Previously in World War II, Japanese scientists performed live blood experiments on American GI prisoners of war, by hanging them from meat hooks under various refrigerated conditions while they studied their blood after purposely being made to bleed to death. This research was then later used in the 1970's to spearhead "American" start-up companies for the production of Interferon (artificial blood) such as the Green Cross Corporation.*-

---

Its experiments in crowd control methods have been widely used on the American public, a surreptitious but nevertheless, outrageous assault on human freedom by modifying individual behavior through topical psychology. A German refugee, Kurt Lewin became the director of Tavistock in 1932. He came to the U.S. in 1933 as a 'refugee', the first of many infiltrators and set up the Harvard Psychology Clinic which originated the propaganda campaign to turn the American public against Germany and involved us in World War II".

"In 1938 Roosevelt executed a secret agreement with Churchill, which in effect, ceded the United States sovereignty to England since it agreed to let Special Operations Executive control U.S. policies. To implement this agreement Roosevelt sent General Donovan to London for indoctrination before setting up OSS (now known as the CIA) under the aegis of SOE – SIS. The entire OSS program as well as the CIA, has always worked on guidelines set up by the Tavistock Institute".

"Tavistock Institute originated the mass civilian bombing raids carried out by Roosevelt and Churchill themselves, **purely as a clinical experiment in mass terror**, keeping records of the results as they watched the 'guinea pigs' reacting under 'controlled laboratory conditions'. **All Tavistock and American foundation techniques have a single goal – 'to break down the psychological strength of the individual and render him or her helpless to oppose dictators of the New World Order'**. Any technique which helps to break down the family unit and family inculcated principles of religion, honor, patriotism and sexual behavior, is used by Tavistock scientists as weapons of crowd control".

"The methods of Freudian psychotherapy **induce permanent, mental illness** in those who undergo this treatment, by **destabilizing their character**. The victim is then advised to 'establish new rituals of personal interaction' that is, to indulge in brief sexual encounters which actually set the participants adrift with no stable, personal relationships in their lives, destroying their ability to establish or maintain a family. Tavistock Institute has developed such power in the U.S., that no one achieves prominence in any field unless they have been trained in behavioral science at Tavistock or one of its subsidiaries".

---

- *__Author's special note__ (JP Cassone'): **This is exactly where "the Western democracies' people" are first most blatantly and outlandishly violated. Instead of their governments enforcing the law to seize and shutdown the individuals behind these "syndicated crime**

**organizations" and have their military intelligence agencies put them under house arrest for "conspiring to commit crimes to endanger and overthrow the State and its citizens", they harbor them! This is the precise location to the cause-of-failure of all Western democracies!**

**Therefore, it can be said under safe assumption that the taxpayers of Western democracies have been financing the ascension of their very own worst enemies who are situated within and above their own governments, ever since the 1920's!** *-

---

"Henry Kissinger, whose meteoric rise to power is otherwise inexplicable, was a German refugee and student of Sir John Rawlings – Reese at SHAEF. Dr. Peter Bourne, a Tavistock Institute psychologist picked Jimmy Carter for President of the U.S., solely because Carter had undergone an intensive brainwashing program administered by Admiral Hyman Rickover at Annapolis. The 'experiment' in compulsory racial integration in the U.S. was organized by Ronald Lippert of the OSS and the American Jewish Congress and Director of Child Training at the Commission on Community Relations. The program was designed to break down the individual's sense of personal knowledge in his identity, his racial heritage. Through the Stanford Research Institute (Menlo Park, CA, USA) Tavistock controls the National Education Association. The Institute of Social Research at the National Training Lab brain-washes the leading executives of business and government".

"Another prominent Tavistock operation is the Wharton School of Finance at the University of Pennsylvania. A single common denominator identifies the common Tavistock strategy – the use of drugs. The infamous MK Ultra program of the CIA in which unsuspecting CIA officials were given LSD and their reaction studied like 'guinea pigs', resulted in several deaths".

"The U. S. government had to pay millions in damages to the families of the victims, but the culprits were never indicted. This program originated when Sandoz AG, a Swiss drug firm owned by S. G. Warburg, Son of Paul Warburg who wrote the Federal Reserve Act and who was the nephew of Max Warburg who had financed Hitler, set up the Institute for Policies Studies to promote the drug. The result was the LSD 'counter culture' of the 1960's, the 'student revolution' which was financed by the CIA for $25 million".

"One part of MK Ultra was the Human Ecology Fund; the CIA also paid Dr. Herbert Kelman of Harvard to carry out further experiments on mind-control. In the 1950's, the CIA financed extensive LSD experiments in Canada. Dr. D Ewen Cameron, president of Canadian Psychological Association and director of Royal Victorian Hospital in Montreal, received huge payments from the CIA to give 53 patients large doses of LSD and record their reactions; the patients were drugged into weeks of sleep and then given electric shock treatments".

"One victim, the wife of a member of the Canadian Parliament, later sued the U.S. companies who provided the drug for the CIA. All the records of the CIA's drug testing programs were ordered destroyed by the head of MK Ultra. Because all efforts of the Tavistock Institute are directed towards producing cyclical collapse the effect of the CIA programs are tragically apparent. R. Emmett Tyrell Jr., writing in the Washington Post August 20, 1984 cites the 'squalid consequences of the 60's radicals in SDS' as resulting in 'the growing rate of illegitimacy, petty lawlessness, drug addiction, welfare, VD and mental illness".

"This is the legacy of the Warburgs and the CIA. Their principal agency the Institute for Policy Studies, was funded by James Paul Warburg; its co-founder was Marcus Raskin, protégé of

McGeorge Bundy, who had Raskin appointed to the post of President Kennedy's personal representative on the National Security Council and in 1963 and funded Students for Democratic Society (the SDS) through which the CIA operated a drug culture".

**"Today the Tavistock Institute operates a $6 billion a year network of foundations in the U.S., all of it funded by U.S. taxpayers' money**. Ten major institutions are under its direct control, with 400 subsidiaries and 3000 other study groups and think tanks which originate many types of programs to increase the control of the World Order over the American People. The Stanford Research Institute adjoining the Hoover Institution, is a $150 million a year operation with 3,300 employees. It carries on program surveillance for Bechtel, Kaiser and 400 other companies and extensive intelligence operations for the CIA. It is the largest institution on the West Coast promoting mind-control and behavioral sciences".

"One of the key agencies as a conduit for secret instructions from Tavistock is the Ditchley Foundation, founded in 1957. The American branch of the Ditchley Foundation is run by Cyrus Vance, former Secretary of State and director of the Rockefeller Foundation and Winston Lord, president of the Council on Foreign Relations". (The letter notes Lord is also a member of Bilderberg and Skull and Bones).

"One of the principal but little known operations of the Rockefeller Foundation has been its techniques for controlling world agriculture. Its director Kenneth Weraimont, set up Rockefeller-controlled agriculture programs throughout Mexico and Latin America. The independent farmer is a great threat to the World Order since he produces for himself and because his produce can be converted into capital which gives him independence. In Soviet Russia the Bolsheviks believed they had attained total control over the people; they were dismayed to find their plans threatened by the stubborn independence of small farmers, the Kulaks".

"Stalin ordered the OGPU to seize all food and animals of the Kulaks and to starve them out. The Chicago American, February 25, 1935 carried a front page headline, 'Six Million Perish in Soviet Famine; Peasants Crops Seized, They and Their Animals Starve'. To draw attention from this atrocity it was later alleged that the Germans and not the Soviet Jews, had killed six million people, the number taken from the Chicago American headline by a Chicago publicist".

"The Communist Party the Party of the Peasants and Worker, exterminated the peasants and enslaved workers. Many totalitarian regimes have found the small farmer to be their biggest stumbling block. The French Reign of Terror was directed, not against the aristocrats, many of whom were sympathetic to it, but against the small farmers who refused to turn over their grain to the revolutionary tribunals, in exchange for the worthless assignats (The French currency of the time). In the United States, the foundations are presently engaged in the same type of war in the extermination of the American farmer".

"The traditional formula of the land plus labor for the farmer has been altered due to the farmer's need for purchasing power, to buy industrial goods needed in his farming operations. Because of this need of capital the farmer is especially vulnerable to the World Order's manipulation of interest rates which is bankrupting him. Just as in the Soviet Union in the early 1930's when Stalin ordered the Kulaks to give up their small plots of land to live and work on the collective farms the American small farmer faces the same type of extermination, being forced to give up his small plot of land to become a hired hand for the big agricultural trusts. *(Reader's note: This is also what is now being implemented in India by its pseudo-multipolar President Pranab Mukherjee's Prime Minister Narendra Modi where an Indian farmer now dies every 30 minutes) The

Brookings Institution and other foundations originated the monetary programs implemented by the Federal Reserve System to destroy the American farmer, a replay of the Soviet tragedy in Russia with one provision that the farmer will be allowed to survive, so long as he becomes a slave worker of the giant trusts".

"Once citizens becomes aware of the true role of the foundations they can understand the high interest rates, high taxes, the destruction of family, the degradation of the churches into forums for revolution, the subversion of the universities into CIA cesspools of drug addiction and the halls of government into sewers of international espionage and intrigue. The American citizen can now understand why every great agent of the federal government is against him; the alphabet agencies, the FBI, CIA, IRS and BATF must make war on the citizen in order to carry out the programs of the foundations".

"The foundations are in direct violation of their charters which commit them to do 'charitable' work, since they make no grants which are not part of a political goal. The charge has been made and never denied, that the Heritage – AEI network has at least two KGB moles on its staff. The employment of professional intelligence operatives as 'charitable' workers was done in the Red Cross Mission to Russia in 1917, exposing the sinister political, economic and social goals which the World Order requires the foundation to achieve through their 'bequests".

**"Not only is this tax fraud, because the foundations are granted tax exemption solely due to charitable work, but it is criminal syndication and conspiracy to commit offenses against the United States, Constitutional Law 213, Corpus Juris Secundum 16**. For the first time, the close interlocking of the foundation's **'syndicate'** has been revealed by the names of its principle incorporators – Daniel Coit Gilman, who incorporated the Peabody Fund and the John Slater Fund and became an incorporator of the General Education Board (now the

Rockefeller Foundation): Gilman also incorporated the Russell Trust in 1856, then later became an incorporator of the Carnegie Institution with Andrew Dickson White (Russell Trust) and Fredric A. Delano, who also was an original incorporator of the Brookings Institution and the Carnegie Endowment for International Peace".

"Daniel Coit Gilman incorporated the Russell Sage Foundation with Cleveland H. Dodge of the National City Bank. These foundations' incorporators have been closely linked to the Federal Reserve System, the War Industries Board of WW I, the OSS of WW II and the CIA. They have also been closely linked with the American International Corporation which was formed to instigate the Bolshevik Revolution in Russia. (As previously mentioned in Chapter IV) Delano, an uncle of Franklin Delano Roosevelt, was on the original Board of Governors of the Federal Reserve System in 1914. His brother-in-law founded the influential Washington Law Firm of Covington and Burling. The Delanos and other ruling families of the World Order have traced their lineage directly back to William of Orange and **the regime** which granted the charter of the Bank of England".

"Tavistock Institutions in the United States are:

**Flow Laboratories**: Gets contracts from the National Institute of Health.

**Merle Thomas Corporation**: Gets contracts from the U.S. Navy and analyzes data from satellites.

**Walden Research**: Does work in the field of pollution control.

**Planning Research Corporation**: Arthur D. Little, G.E. 'Tempo', Operations Research Inc. Part of approximately 350 firms who conduct research and surveys for making recommendations to government. They are part of what **President Eisenhower called, 'a possible danger to public policy that could itself become captive of a scientific-technological elite'**.

**Brookings Institution**: Dedicates its work to what it calls a 'national agenda'. Wrote President Hoover's program, President Roosevelt's 'New Deal', the Kennedy Administration's 'New Frontiers' program and President Johnson's 'Great Society'. (As also mentioned previously in Chapter IV) **Brookings has been telling the United States government how to conduct its affairs for the past 70 years and is still doing so.**

**Hudson Institute**: This institution has done more to shape the way Americans react to political and social events, think, write and generally conduct themselves than perhaps any, except the 'Big Five'.

*(Reader's Note: **1**-Openness, **2**-Conscientiousness, **3**-Extraversion/Introversion, **4**-Agreeableness and **5**-Natural Reactions constitute 'The Big Five'. It was first named by Lewis Goldberg, a researcher at the Oregon Research Institute. The Big Five, or Five-Factor Model of Personality traces its roots back to 1936 where researchers Allport and Odbert were the first researchers to identify the trait-descriptive words in the English language. From 1954 – 1961, two Airforce personnel researchers Tupes and Christal (1961), became the first researchers to make use of Allport and Odberts' work by then establishing "The Big Five").

“Hudson Institute specialized in defense policy research and the relations with the former USSR. Most of its military work is classified as Secret. Hudson may be properly classified as one of ‘Committee of 300’s’ brain-washing establishments. One of its largest clients is the U.S. Department of Defense which includes matters of civil defense, national security, military policy and arms control”.

*(Reader’s note: Associated with the “Delphi Techniques” of future forecasting, the techniques were first hatched by researchers Herman Kahn and Olaf Helmer at the Rand Corporation. Later Kahn left Rand to form the Hudson Institute, while Helmer went on to co-found the Institute for the Future, which is located within close proximity to both the Stanford Research Institute and Facebook’s headquarters. As a writer who’s always concerned for his reader’s mental safety, any of you whom currently are ‘Facebook users’ should be made aware that this organization, along with its nearby associate institutions, are all heavily interrelated in their involvement with both the U.S. Department of Defense and “mind-control” practices!)

"Hudson Institute gave us GOALS 2000 and authored the Freedom From Religious Persecution Act which became the International Religious Freedom Act of 1998. This law requires the creation of a federal commission to monitor religion chaired by a presidentially-appointed Ambassador-at-Large on International Religious Freedom under the mandates of the United Nations' covenants and authority of the International Criminal Court".

**National Training Laboratories**: "One of the key institutions established for this purpose in the United States. NTL was founded in 1947 by members of the Tavistock network in the United States and located originally on an estate in Bethel, Maine. NTL has as its explicit purpose, the brain-washing of leaders of government, educational institutions and corporate bureaucracies in Tavistock methods and then using these 'leaders' to either themselves, run Tavistock group sessions in their organizations, or to hire other similar trained group leaders to do the job. The 'nuts and bolts' of the NTL operations revolves around the particular form of Tavistock **degenerative psychology** known as 'group dynamics', developed by German Tavistock operative Kurt Lewin, who emigrated to the United States in the 1930's and whose students founded NTL".

"In a Lewinite brain-washing group, a number of individuals from various backgrounds and personalities, are manipulated by a 'group leader' to form a 'consensus' of opinion, achieving a new 'group identity'. The key to the process is the creation of a controlled environment, in which stress is introduced (sometimes called 'dissonance') **to crack an individual's belief structure**. *(Reader's note: Can you believe that America's taxpayers actually support these criminally insane and conspiring enemies-of-the-State, sadomasochists?) Using the peer pressure of other group members, the individual is 'cracked' and a new personality emerges with new values. This degrading experience causes the person to deny that any changes have taken place. In that way, an individual is brain-washed without the victim knowing what has taken place".

"This method is the same with some minor modifications as the ones used in all so-called 'sensitivity groups', or 'T-groups', or in the more extreme case, 'drug-sex-and rock & roll' culture form and 'touchy-feely groups', such as the kind popularized from the 1960's onward by the Esalen Institute which was set up with the help of the NTL. From the mid-1950's onward NTL put the majority of the nation's corporate leadership through such brain-washing programs while running similar programs for the State Department, the Navy, the Department of Education and other sections of the federal bureaucracy. There is no firm estimate of the number of Americans who have been put through this process over the past 40 years at either the NTL, or as it is now known as the National Training Laboratories Institute for Applied Behavioral Sciences based in Rosslyn, Virginia, or at its West Coast base of operations at the Western Training Laboratories in Group Development, or in various satellite institutions".

"One of the groups that went through the NTL mill in the 1950's was the leadership of the National Education Association (NEA), the largest organization of teachers in the United States. Thus, the NEA's outlook has been shaped by Tavistock through the NTL. In 1964 (the year following Kennedy's assassination) the NTL Institute became a direct part of the NEA with the NTL setting up 'group sessions' for all its affiliates **with funding from the Department of Education**. The NTL Institute drafted the programs for the training of the nation's primary and secondary school teachers and has a hand as well, in developing the content of educational 'reforms', including OBE". *(Reader's note: OBE, or "Outcome Based Education" was spearheaded by Benjamin Bloom and was derived from B.F. Skinner's "Mastery Learning")

"Also known as the International Institute for Applied Behavioral Sciences, this institute is a brain-washing center in ‘artificial stress training’ where participants suddenly find themselves against vicious accusations. While officially decrying ‘racism’, it is interesting to note that NTL working with NEA, produced a paper proposing vouchers which would separate the hard-to-teach children from the brighter ones and funding would be allocated according to the number of difficult children who would be separated. The proposal was not taken up”.

**University of Pennsylvania’s Wharton School of Finance and Commerce**: (*Reader’s note: Do not permit yourself to be intimidated by this institution’s title. Today it has sunken into being not much beyond a bunch of overly glorified white-collar gangsters in academia who teach people how to “legally lie” within the professions of economy and accounting. This explains why its popular street name has now been reduced to “The School of Cooked-book Economics” or “The School of the Banksters’ Gangsters”! ) “Founded by Eris Trist, one of the ‘brain trusts’ of Tavistock, Wharton has become one of the more important Tavistocks in so far as ‘Behaviorial Research’ is concerned. Wharton attracts clients such as the U.S. Department of Labor (USDL) – which teaches how to produce ‘cooked book’ statistics *(Reader’s note: Translated meaning, accounting and statistical tracking methods of “how to legally lie-and-deceive”) at the Wharton Econometric Forecasting Associates Incorporated. This method was very much in demand as we came to the close of 1991 with millions more out of work than was reflected in the USDL statistics. Wharton’s ‘Econometric Modeling’ is used by every major company within the ‘Committee of 300’ in the United States, Western Europe, The International Monetary Fund (IMF), the United Nations and the World Bank. The Institute for Social Research is among its clients, as well as the Ford Foundation, the U.S. Department of Defense (DOD), the U.S. Postal Service (USPS) and the U.S. Department of Justice. Among its studies are ‘The Human Meaning of Social Change’, ‘Youth in Transition’ and ‘How American’s View their Mental Health”.

**Institute for the Future**: "This is not a typical Tavistock institution, in that it is funded by the Ford Foundation, yet it draws its long-range forecasting from the mother of all think tanks. Institute for the Future projects what it believes to be changes that will be taking place in the time frames of fifty years. So-called 'Delphi Panels' decide what is normal and what is not and prepare position papers to 'steer' government in the right direction, to head-off such groups as 'people creating civil disorder'. *(Reader's note: This could be patriotic groups demanding the abolition of graduated taxes, or demanding that their rights to bear arms is not be infringed upon). This institute recommends actions such as liberalizing abortion laws, drug usage and that cars entering an urban area pay tolls, teaching birth control in public schools, requiring registration of firearms, making the use of drugs a non-criminal offense, legalizing homosexuality, paying students for scholastic achievements, making zoning controls a preserve of the State, offering bonuses for family planning and last and most frightening, a Pol Pot Cambodia-type styled proposal that new communities be establish in rural areas (*Readers note: Translated meaning, 'concentration camps or compounds'). As can be observed, many of their goals have already been more than fully realized".

**Institute for Policy Studies**: "IPS has shaped and reshaped United States policies both foreign and domestic, since it was founded by James P. Warburg and the Rothschild entities in the United States. Its networks in America include the League for Industrial Democracy. Lead players in this organization have included Jeane Kirkpatrick former U.S. Ambassador to the United Nations, Irwin Suall of the Anti-defamation League (ADL)Eugene Rostow Arms Control negotiator, Lane Kirkland labor leader and Albert Shankier. IPS was incorporated in 1963 by Marcus Raskin and Richard Barnett, both highly trained Tavistock graduates. The objectives of IPS came from an agenda laid down for it by the Tavistock Institute, one of the most notable being to create the 'New

Left' as a grass roots movement in the U.S. *(Reader's note: Before the Bolshevik Revolution in Russia, Stalin's Jewish Lieutenants used similar propaganda techniques for luring and identifying the disloyal, while instigating unrest to extract dissidents.) It's been said that Barnett and Raskin controlled such diverse elements as the Black Panthers, Daniel Ellsberg, National Security staff member Halprin, The Weathermen Underground, the Venceramos and the campaign of presidential candidate George McGovern. No scheme was too big for the IPS and its controllers to take and manage".

"Throughout its many lobbying groups on Capitol Hill, IPS relentlessly used its 'Big Stick' to beat Congress. IPS has a network of lobbyists all supposedly operating independently, but in actual fact acting cohesively, so that Congresspersons are pummeled from all sides by seemingly different and varied lobbyists. In this way IPS was and still is able to successfully sway the individual Representatives and Senators to vote for 'what's trending' and in IPS's favor. By using key point-men on Capitol Hill, IPS was able to break into the very infrastructure of the U.S. legislative system and the way it works".

"IPS became and remains to this day, to be one of the most prestigious 'think tanks' controlling foreign policy decisions, which 'we the people' foolishly believe are those of our lawmakers. By sponsoring militant activism at home and with links to revolutionaries abroad and by engineering such victories as the 'The Pentagon Papers', besieging the corporate structure, bridging the credibility gap between unground movements and acceptable political activism, by penetrating religious organizations and using them to sow discord in America, such as radical and racial policies, under the guise of religion, using establishment media to spread IPS ideas and then supporting them, IPS has lived up to the role in which it was designed for". *(Reader's note: Translated meaning, 'another contingency conduit' of the New World Order's destabilization agenda, or as they might prefer it in this case, 'organized and controlled chaos'.)

"Grants for the IPS came from the Samuel Rubin Foundation and the Stern Family Fund. Samuel Rubin was himself a member of the elite Comintern of the Communist Party, founded by none other than Lenin himself. Billionaire Armond Hammer assisted Rubin in making the fortunes which helped launch IPS. Philip Stern, an IPS trustee, was the president of the Stern Fund. The Executive Director of the Stern Fund, Dabvid R. Hunter, was previously an official of the National Council and World Council of Churches".

**Stanford Research Institute** (SRI): "Jessie Hobson, the first president of the Stanford Research Institute in a 1952 speech made it clear what lines the institute was to follow. Stanford can be described as one of the 'jewels' in Tavistock's crown in its rule over the United States. Founded in 1946 immediately after the close of WW II, it was presided over by Charles A. Anderson with emphasis on 'mind control' research and 'future sciences'. Included under the Stanford umbrella was the Charles F. Kittering Foundation which developed the 'Changing Images of Man', upon which the Aquarian Conspiracy rests". *(Reader's note: "The Aquarian Conspiracy" was coined and made famous by writer Marilyn Ferguson's 1980 book of the same name.)

"Some of Stanford's major clients and contracts were at first centered around the defense establishment but as Stanford grew, so did the diversity of its services which is glaringly evident by just the following sampling: applications of Behavioral Sciences to Research Management Office of Science and Technology, SRI Business and Intelligence Program, U.S. Department of Defense Directorate of Defense Research and Engineering and the U.S. Department of Defense Office of Aerospace Research. Among corporations seeking Stanford's services are Wells Fargo, the Bechtel Corporation, Hewlett Packard, Bank of America, McDonnell Douglas, Blyth, Eastman Dillion and TRW. One of Stanford's more secret projects was extensive work on chemical and bacteriological warfare weapons" (CAB).

"Stanford Research is plugged into at least 200 smaller 'think tanks' doing research in every facet of life in America. This is ARPA networking and represents the emergence of probably the most far reaching effort to control the environment of every individual in the country. At present, Stanford's computers are linked with 2,500 'sister' research consoles which include the CIA, Bell Labs, U.S. Army Intelligence, Office of Naval Intelligence (ONI), Rand, MIT, Harvard and UCLA. Stanford plays a key role in that it is 'the library' cataloging all ARPA's documentation".

"One can use one's imagination here when saying 'other agencies' are allowed to search through SRI's 'library' for key words and phrases, look through sources and update their own master files with those of the Stanford Research Center. The Pentagon uses SRI's master files extensively and there is little doubt that other U.S. government agencies do the same. The Pentagon's 'Command and Control' problems are workout out by Stanford".

"Though these applications only pertain to weapons and soldiers, there is absolutely no guarantee that the same research could not and will not be turned into civilians applications. Stanford is known to be willing to do anything for anyone".

**Massachusetts Institute of Technology (MIT), Alfred P. Sloan School of Management**: "This major institute is not generally recognized as being part of Tavistock U.S.A. Most people look upon it as being purely an American Institution, but that is far from the truth. MIT-Alfred Sloan can be roughly divided into the following groups: Contemporary Technology Industrial Relations NASA-ERC Computer Research Laboratories, Office of Naval Research Group and Psychology Systems Dynamics. Some of MIT's clients are: American Management Association, Committee for Economic Development, GTE, Institute for Defense Analysis (IDA),

NASA, National Academy of Sciences, National Council of Churches, Sylvania, TRW, U.S. Army, U.S. State Department, the U.S. Navy, U.S. Treasury Department and Volkswagen Corporation".

**Rand Research and Development Corporation**: "Without a doubt RAND is the think tank most beholden to the Tavistock Institute and is the vehicle for control of United States policies at every level. Specific RAND policies that became operative, including America's ICBM's (Inter-Continent ballistic Missiles system), prime analysis for U.S. foreign policy making, instigator of space programs, U.S. nuclear policies, corporate analysis, hundreds of projects for the military and the CIA in relations to the use of mind-altering drugs in the covert MK Ultra operation lasting some 20 years".

"Herman Kahn, the founder of RAND also found the Hudson Institute in 1961. In "Educating for the New World Order" B.K. Eakman tells of a training manual with a 1971 U.S. Office of Education contract number on it entitled, "Training for Change Agents"; seven volumes of "change agent studies" commissioned by the Office of Education to the Rand Corporation in 1973 – 1974. Scores of other papers submitted by behaviorist researchers who had obtained grants from the U.S. Office of Education for the purpose of exploring ways to 'freeze' and 'unfreeze' values, 'to implement change' and to turn potentially hostile groups and committees into acquiescent, rubber-stamp bodies by means of such strategies as the 'Delphi Technique".

"Some of RAND's clients include AT & T, Chase Manhattan Bank, IBM, the National Science Foundation, the Republican Party, TRW, the U.S. Airforce, U.S. Department of Health and the U.S. Department of Energy".

"RAND was once accused of being commissioned by the USSR, to work out terms of surrender of the United States government, an accusation took it all the way to the U.S. Senate, where it was taken up by Senator Symington and subsequently fell victim to scorn poured out by the establishment press. 'Brain-washing' remains the primary function of RAND". (END OF LETTER) –

In the eyes of God once hoisted upon the scales of democracy, truth, freedom, sovereignty, ethics, morality, virtue, loyalty, honesty, and sensibility, this nation of the United States lay stripped naked of each and every one of these. As Genghis Khan had proven that "no one race is exceptional, no one bloodline is deserving of privilege", so too Solomon had proven that "excessive wealth and power, knows no contentment".

Western civilization lies bound and gagged, taken hostage by the ones needing the most amount of control, now in control of the ones needing it the least. Ever buried and suffocating, its morbid body now lies beneath the vile heaps of tyrannical prestige, affluent corruption and rapacious deceit of its institutionalized conspiracies and contemptuous crime syndicates. This all being administered by the handlers of infiltrating rulers, who have broken every bone in liberty's body and shattered every pane of love to its will.

The West is a barren, lost wasteland, a cemetery from ear to ear and a travesty beyond all comprehension. In the destitution of its reflection, it is a monumental example to each and every nation outside, of everything what not to be. Time quickly fleets the West, as its doors to an unstained world outside forever quarantine this vulgar pandemic of an old world disorder.

# Chapter XI

## Leave NATO or Die

There is an endless list of very sound-thinking, seasoned, geopolitical journalists and astute, investigative writers and historians found within the alternative news sector. They come from all walks of life with people such as Ostrovsky, Coleman and Cooper who worked within the Mossad, MI6 and US Naval Intelligence. What they have known, did and do they perform or had performed, exceptionally well.

I could take the best half dozen of them, have each one explain and layout for you in every facet of how the world works today and the barebones truth of what's "actually" happening behind the scenes, with supporting evidence to every single aspect of their findings, in the finest detail. And once I did this, what would you do? Would you live any differently? Would you make any changes in your life? What made you buy, or at least read this book? The point I'm trying to reach here is that although I'm privy to all these reliable sources of information, I must keep things in perspective of the common citizen in laymen's terms, so as not to have you overwhelmed with TMI (Too much information).

(Balkans protest NATO)

To become more informed so that it connects you with an understanding which was once only half understood before is fine. But I wish to make clear, I am in no way ever condoning, nor promoting dissent or revolution in what I write.

Gordon Duff, editor of Veterans Today and former combat Marine veteran of the Vietnam War recently stated in an article from Beijing, "Why does the world have to become concerned about American politics? The answer is simple, if you are going to die in your home with your family torn to pieces around you, chances are it will be America killing you".

The West of today is being ruled by some very demented people. Their neoliberals are killing people in foreign countries while its conservative ideologues think they're not killing enough. The invasion of Iraq was planned three and half years prior to "The 9-11 Incident". The West's neocons set their program for removing 7 governments in five years. Since 9-11 Washington has destroyed eight countries.

(Bavaria protests NATO)

Germany and the UK continue to act as neutered vassal States of Washington, complacent to the chances of a nuclear war. The majority of the free world and of the West's own citizens, are begging for just one European State with a backbone, to stand erect and exit NATO. Just one Greece, one Spain, one Italy, or one France and a stampede to leave NATO would ensue and along with it a vacuum of Western hegemony and the war machine. Dr. Paul Craig Roberts, former U.S. Assistant Treasury Secretary recently stated it poignantly, "As long as Europe remains nothing but an extension of Washington, the prospect for Armageddon will continue to rise".

And for those of you who consider yourselves of the expert level of geopolitics who CGEI (Can't get enough information), here's the longhand version. The elitist criminality that has sought sanctuary within the 51 syndicate organizational members inside The Conference of Presidents of Major American Jewish Organizations, Israel, the Israeli government, or as rogue CIA and Mossad operatives, the Clinton Foundation, the offices of McCain, Romney, Bush and the Salinas cartel, have now spread throughout our industries and into Wall Street, the diamond markets, currency markets, banking system, Federal Reserve, Treasury Department, policy think tanks and Western military complexes. These are the very actual "real terrorists of humankind", not Arabs, not Muslims, not small farmers, not independent thinkers, and certainly not independent journalists or columnists. This menacing elite crime cabal has a stranglehold which enjoys no oversight, no

(Greece protests NATO)

investigations and no indictments, permitted freely to threaten, extort, blackmail and/or strongly coerce the many members of the U.S. House and Senate who now spin their wheels and push their buttons in attempts to get a major World War started, as it all comes boiling down into a triplication of fear. The fear in their dreams that their chances of reigning supreme over a globally

(Turkey protests NATO)

blanketed police State is quickly slipping away. The fear of them losing control of Eurasia and its routes of trade and the fear that no matter how much money they are throwing in all directions, the world has flatly rejected and is denying their New World Disorder. The people are patiently waiting, they are waiting to bury them, bury them forever to be forgotten and with good riddance! No Mrs. Clinton, you're all not losing the "information war" you're all losing your minds! The European governments are soon to be classified insane as well.

Think about this, the EU economy was on the brink of seeing green shoots and a robust recovery through Russian trade. Then Washington change the video to their matrix and screamed, "We will not dismantle NATO, we will expand it and implement Cold War 2.0" to which the European leadership all bowed down as cowering lapdogs. So Europe blindly kissed their Eastern imports good-bye, along with many jobs and traded it all for a spike in defense spending and budget deficits, so as only to line the pockets of their ruling criminal elite. Then Washington screamed again, "Sanctions" to which European leaders once again bowed as cowering lapdogs as they kissed their Eastern exports good-bye, leaving their farmers knee deep in rotting produce. And then Washington yet again came screaming, “Bomb Syria”, to which European leaders as cowering lapdogs obeyed and became inundated with swarms of refugees and the loss of even more jobs with even higher deficits.

(Spain protests NATO)

Then Russia exposed to the world in video detail, the Washington support of ISIS and other terrorists in Syria as well as illegal oil smuggling the exact same offense I might add, that they hung Saddam Hussein for. Oh but you see this crime was committed by "a NATO member" (Turkey). This all leaves Europe shivering on the dark side of the moon. "Wake-up leaders of Europe, hello; is anybody in there"?

Washington's power-crazed, exceptionally fanatical neocons and neoliberals' had planned for a regime change in Syria which blew up in their faces and in the process they have now fully destabilized Europe. There is always the remote chance that they will become so reckless that Washington accidently attacks itself. Say, now there's a country worthy of regime changing, don't you think? Well anyway, getting back to Europe's leadership. Just when you thought they had reached the bottom of subservience in boot licking and tail kissing, Washington came screaming yet even again with, "Be my door mat to death in a nuclear war", to which European leaders again stooped as cowering lapdogs and will become extinct toast with an irretraceable history. Does anyone in Europe's government bodies grow balls?

(Belgium protests NATO)

If at a later date in time, what I've mentioned in this book should be blamed for causing riots in Europe, or even India I stand corrected. You see after all I owe Europeans a deep apology. There's not much wrong with the world's citizenry in the West it's the criminal elite inside its ruling classes. If riots should come of it, it'll be because they've all been harboring inside, everything I've been saying up to this point. Let's face it, if you don't shutdown the range after you've boiled the water it will overflow!

This past year the criminal acts committed by the West for regime change in "democracy-based countries" is surpassing the Third Reich's extent of crimes and demeanor. Sabre-rattling Russia, China, Yemen, Syria, Iran and Brazil, just to scratch the surface, is broadcasting to the world that Washington is in deep denial,

(China protests NATO)

desperately seeking a grand diversion to having to face the music back home in economics. However now extreme and berserk, its network press still remains stuck in the mud of its usual cover-up fashion in shifting out the atrocities, the psychotic froth and all the psychopathic elements, not to mention the long list of international law violations, treaty violations, human rights violations and its endless array of numerous crimes against humanity. What most would like to know in all of this is "where was the U.N."? Where was it after the bombing of the Chinese Embassy, of Belgrade, the start of illegal oil-price rigging and the manipulation of the Russian ruble, NATO's expansionism, the China A shares rigging, the illegal coup in Kiev, the West's numerous violations in both surveillance and conduct in the South China sea, the downing of the Su-24, the covert, illicit undermining in Venezuela, Brazil and Bolivia and the recorded video coverage of Israeli – U.S. support to ISIS officers, supplies and stolen oil transports? If the U.N.'s 70th anniversary demonstrates it has flat out failed its Charter's objectives, let's have last rights performed now, liquidate its headquarters and disperse the proceeds to the taxpayers!

(Croatia protests NATO)

When an exodus caused by primarily 6,000 Western sorties purposely being dropped on dud targets, causing one million refugees to show up on the EU's doorstep, the high-level emergency response committee's meetings of this so-called glorious Union of Europe all ended with no cohesive response, viable plan, or expressed solutions. I would consider this 28 member puppy both dead and useless! The Western civilizations today are seen with their citizenry bound and gagged as the momentum to its slide increases from a do-nothing Congress and a do-nothing Parliament, to a do-nothing U.N. with a do-nothing EU. Their only responses keep repeating, "Oh God forbid that we just have peace".

The unlawful interference into the Arab country of Syria by the EU now begins to unravel its own bloc at home in a rapid rise of anti-NATO, anti-emigration and anti-EU consensus, especially in the UK, France, Denmark, the Netherlands and Belgium. Britain, France and the U.S. have given support to insurgency against a democratically elected government (Syria) by aiding and abetting Al-Qaeda, the Islamic State of IS, ISIS, ISIL and whatever the hell else they're going to be called next and radical mercenary extremists. Russia, Iran and Lebanon are the only legal and lawful

(Czech Republic protests NATO)

contingency in Syria, having been requested and approved by Syria's government. The only offenders in violation of international law here are the very Western nations who themselves, spearheaded the very laws into the statutes!

(France protests NATO)

Russian President Vladimir Putin, after extending the olive branches until none remained on the tree, has been received with no avail from the warmongering, scoundrel West and was left with no alternatives but to sign the new “About the Strategy of National Security of the Russian Federation”, this 2016 New Year’s Eve. In the highlight of rising tensions the document for the first time, named the United States as a threat to Russia’s National Security. The document which replaces the 2009 version, serves as a basis for a planning strategy relating to national security. The 2009 version did not mention the United States.

(Wales protests NATO)

The U.S. is accused in the new document, of expanding its network of military-biological laboratories in countries neighboring Russia. "The strengthening of Russia happens against a background of new threats to the national security which has complex and interrelated nature", the document states. Russia's efforts to maintain an independent, international and domestic policy says the document, had caused "counteraction from the U.S. and its allies which are striving to retain their dominance in global affairs". The document also mentions "Expansion of NATO" as a threat to Russia's national security.

Any country in the world which is now hosting a U.S. military base is also providing a means for the U.S. to develop war materials and has just made themselves a nuclear target. The eventual "expulsions of U.S. bases" from various countries in the aftermath of this new Russian document would not come as a surprise to a world community already weary of hearing one too many reports of Washington's latest hegemonic atrocities.

*****

*__Author's Interjection__: Allow me to take a brief and minor diversion here in the hopes of better explaining what is causing these sudden groundswells of "the new warring factor" permeating throughout the Western democracies. Thomas Jefferson once stated, "I have seen enough of one war, never to wish to see another". This statement is also very much representative of the general consensus in all citizenry since they are the ones who will have to fight them. As previously mentioned in my book "Tandem", author Michael Rivero was quoted as saying, "All wars are Banker's Wars" which is also the title of his great book. The reason for the very American Revolution itself and the founding of the United States was in rebellion against King George III's "Currency Act" of 1763 which forbid all settlements to be made with any currency other than the bank notes issued by the Bank of England which generated interest payments to the banks.

Just when the first Americans thought they had all the bankers licked by winning the American Revolutionary War, along came Mayer Amschal Rothschild. Through the tyrannical and conspiring acts of using Alexander Hamilton as his front man (he's on $5 U.S. bill) in 1791 the first private Central Bank was set up in the U.S. called The First Bank of the United States. By the end of its first twenty years in operation it had almost succeeded in completely destroying the entire U.S. economy to enrich the bankers. Throughout our last 300 years of history scores of ethical, highly respected men have been gunned down or assassinated soon after they made challenges to this elite Crime Syndicate known as the Central Bankers! In reality they are not a very large group of individuals who will someday be completely exterminated by a combined global force but until that day arrives, Western democracies are yet held hostage to these central banking schemes.

After the Vietnam War there existed absolutely no cause for a war in the Middle East, the United States, Europe or Russia. So Menachem Begin and his Jewish-extremist cohorts invented "terrorism". Shortly to follow were the pro-terror neocons of Jewish extremists Robert Kagan, co-founder of Project for the New

American Century and The Foreign Policy Initiative, whose think-tank members greatly assisted in engineering "The 9-11 Event" and the Iraq wars. As an added bonus to the Central Banking Cabal and putting the world a step closer to Armageddon was Kagan's wife, U.S. Assistant Secretary of State Victoria Nuland, nicknamed "The Cookie Monster" who assisted in engineering the Ukrainian coup and has been popularized by her reoccurring, boldfaced lies and propaganda about why we should hate and escalate wars.

According to Harvard economist Linda Bilmes, both the Afghanistan and Iraq wars alone have cost U.S. taxpayers some $4 to $6 trillion. The Crime Syndicate of the Central Banking establishment shall always demand a steady stream of constant and continuous "wars, murders and mayhem" in order to sustain its bottomless appetite.

I am an individual who calls things as he sees them. I do "not" believe that everyone in the CIA, the U.S. State Department, U.S. Naval Intelligence, the entire upper brass of Western military officers, etc., or even the Mossad or MI6 are all bad or corrupt. Once a unified, global force starting from within these organizations to other domestic government branches and its foreign allies' and yes, even its multipolar rivals, can all unite in a concerted front with an inclusive grassroots movement against this banking establishment, have them taken out, executed and put to death with all assets seized and redistributed back into the global system as "peaceful, coexisting nations", the ox-yokes of debt will completely be removed from the global economy and the world will know "the 1,000 years of peace"!

During the 1300's King Phillip IV of France once discovered a similar group of elitist criminals who were once bleeding his nation and the world dry and who hid under the auspices of The Knights Templar. He then proceeded to round up 900 of them, seized their assets and had them swiftly burned at the stake! So yes, this united global front taking action would likely entail seizing prominent individuals, a high percentage of certain families, government departmental members, entire financial business such as Goldman Sachs and perhaps even many U.S. media networks who might have been guilty of collusion, but such are the circumstances when taking down a worldwide criminal super-syndicate. Its time and evolution has now delivered us all upon the front stoops of "one final Fate". If you have any second thoughts just reconsider what type of world these mongrels have delivered just the American democracy alone, by familiarizing yourself with some of these excerpts I had made mention of earlier in "Tandem":

The U.S. government is so in debt its money is soon to become worthless. In less than 2 years there will be a great market crash, 6 x's worse than the Great Depression. The U.S. government "gold vaults" are empty. Only places like China, Russia and those countries who have ample gold supplies on hand will survive this catastrophe.

The U.S. is now:

- #1 in the amount of people in jail.

- #1 in obesity.

- #1 in amount of television watched.

- #1 in divorce.

- #1 in illegal drug use.

- #1 in auto thefts.

- #1 in murder.

- #1 in amount of police officers.

- #1 in total crimes.

- #1 in spending on healthcare.

- #1 in people on pharmaceutical drugs.

- #1 in number of women taking anti-depressants.

- #1 in student loan debts.

- #1 in rape.

- #1 in the most complicated tax system.

- #1 in national debt.

Americans are 7 x's more likely to be shot by their own police officers than they are a terrorist and the U.S. government debt grows at a rate of $40,000-per-second.

All of humanity has now arrived at this final fork in the road. Either take these necessary, just and united steps in a unified front to takeout this global crime syndicate now in the name of perpetual peace, or have every living thing end up in pieces from an Armageddon nuclear war.

*****

(Ireland protests NATO)

Campaign for Nuclear Disarmament (CND) is currently seeking Britain to leave NATO and oppose its expansion. Operating on a global scale NATO has become an ever-expanding interventionist bloc, contrary to its founding principles and in the contemporary model demonstrates a complete disregard for the rule of law. If "law" is needed anywhere to be adhered to, it is in the "nuclear sense". Just one example of its destabilizing and destructive disposition would be in Afghanistan where it protects "someone's" supply of the world's heroine poppy fields with American soldiers whose number one cause of death is now suicide. NATO disregarded the hard earned Non-Proliferation Treaty achieved by both Reagan and Gorbachov and has proceeded to keep deploying nuclear weapons in Germany, Italy and Belgium. Also assigned to NATO is Britain's Trident nuclear weapons system.

NATO was originally established in 1949, during the early years of Cold War 1.0. After the fall of the Berlin Wall in 1989 the time had come to dissolve NATO as was done with the Warsaw Pact in 1991. But in Washington certain Zionist-Jewish extremists gave birth to a very dangerous ideology. Instead of constructive and economic engagement and collaboration with Russia, Washington's extremists hijacked United States' policy, cemented its feet to the unipole and reignited a new Cold War 2.0 which no one had any interest in. It is as if after a super bowl game the winning team chose to "move in and live at that stadium permanently" and every day which followed it just gets up and keeps singing "we are the champions, we are the champions", as it completely ignores the pleas from crowds of people who keep approaching them repeatedly yelling, "Ah, its game-over guys, time to go home", again and again to no avail.

Germany and France the larger of the Euro minions, along with the Czech Republic, Greece, Italy, Spain and Ireland have become doubting and hesitant on the way of sanctions. They are starting to feel real hurt. There is also a concern of new geopolitical talk making the rounds in Europe that Washington's Menachem Begin-like, Jewish-terrorists known for their "Lavon Affair" stencil trademark of igniting false-flag events to have them falsely appear being committed by someone else, is planning to stage a most horrific biological weapons explosion or the silent, slow-release of similar ingredients onto the European populations, where 100,000 or more will die and have this incident all window dressed to blame it on Russia. This is the extent to which the United States' handlers have now reached.

So this now gluttonous, headless behemoth NATO has Washington recently demanding all the member nations must now contribute a full 2% of their GDP to defense. It even included Greece, who was on the brink of fiscal collapse at this printing. When NATO official Jens Stoltenberg was approached about this issue he replied that he still expects Greece to continue spending the full 2% of its GDP on defense.

Italy must allocate an average of "52 million euros-per-day" to military spending, according to official data of NATO itself and as a NATO member. That figure is calculated by the Stockholm

(Sicily protests NATO)

International Institute for Peace Research, to actually be greater than the “72 million euros-per-day”. Within the framework of the Alliance the Italian government may well yet have to increase that figure again to “100 million euros-per-day”! NATO and its EU governments are robbing the public’s funds of all quality social, health, education and retirement reserves to an alliance whose strategy proclaims itself defensive, while it hijacks the Alliance’s agenda to the offensive posturing.

The North Atlantic Council approved the “New Strategic Concept” at a 1999 summit in Washington which basically transforms NATO into an alliance for carrying out military aggression. With the wars in Yugoslavia (1999), Afghanistan (2001 – 2015) and Libya (2011), plus the actions to destabilize Ukraine in alliance with local Fascist forces, this new strategy was put into effect. The “New Strategic Concept” violates all principles of the U.N. Charter. “Hey, U.N.; where in the hell are you”?

(The Netherlands protests NATO)

By leaving NATO Italy would remove itself from this strategy of "permanent war" which violates the Italian Constitution, in particular of Article 11 and damages Italy's real national interests. The Italian Republic is deprived of its ability to make autonomous choices under NATO membership. Whoever is currently controlling NATO they are "acting as every citizen of the NATO Alliance's nations' #1 enemy, advancing completely against their will"! This pits European citizens in alliance with Russia, China and Syria against their own governments! Why? "Who the hell else is listening to them"? Certainly not the Jewish-extremists' television networks in Washington. It is identical to the Third Reich's Nazi playbook; "perpetual war with no economic plans, or intentions for a peace time economy"! Hitler had only planned for his soldier's children to continue the wars and their children to continue the wars. Italy cannot shape freely its foreign and military policy, democratically adopted by Parliament on the basis of Constitutional principles.

The Supreme Allied Commander in Europe, NATO's highest military post, is always an American U.S. General appointed by the President of the United States. All other key NATO commands are all assigned to senior U.S. officers. Therefore, NATO is under the command of the United States with the Unites States under the command of extremist, Zionist Jews which uses it (much like they utilized ISIS) as their tool to advance their own military, political and economic ambitions.

(Poland protests NATO)

Italy's NATO membership reinforces its subjection to the United States as exemplified by the network of U.S. – NATO military bases on Italian territory which has transformed Italy into a sort of U.S. aircraft carrier in the Mediterranean. Particularly serious is the presence of U.S. nuclear bombs at these bases which Italian pilots are being trained in their use, forcing Italy to violate the Nuclear Non-Proliferation Treaty which its own government already signed and ratified. By becoming neutral and leaving NATO Italy would recover a substantial amount of its sovereignty and be able to act as a bridge of peace towards South and East. "Does anyone in the Italian Parliament grow balls"?

2015 was the 70th anniversary of the end of WW II when Nazism and Eurofascism were defeated. This would not have been possible without Russia. Ironically, during the commemorations to this historic event in Moscow, not one of the political leaders from the U.S., Britain, France, or other EU member States, were in attendance. This is not only the highest order of back-stabbing, sacrilegious and scurrilous disrespect, but it projects glaring evidence to the world that the new Zionist Jew-extremists are without a doubt "the return of a Fascist Empire who now, unequivocally controls both the Washington government as well as that of the EU nations". It is "Hitler reborn" only this time he's going to take us all with him! Must history repeat itself yet again on this? Are the U.S. and EU extremist politicians in their blood lust of international barbarism, actually capable to stop and make a realization?

(Serbia protests NATO)

Through intentional manipulations of all policy and past treaties and through rehearsed acts of division and campaigns of a frothing pressititude press to hate, to distrust, to commit antitrust and to instill fear the Western civilizations are being conditioned to die. To die in an unnecessary nuclear war, against their will and to be consumed in the destruction of all life on both sides, all because “men without balls and a backbone just sat there, fearful to do anything and allowed it to all happen”!

# Chapter XII

## The New World Order is a Levon Affair

The contemporary West's superficial means of using "perpetual war" and "nuclear blackmail" seem a necessary component to their procedural agenda of looting the planet, acquiring incomprehensible wealth and power, while achieving the ability to crush all challenges in keeping it. The Bilderberg Group, the Council on Foreign Relations (CFR), the Trilateral Commission, and the Zionist dystopia connects all the dots.

The CFR in the U.S. is dominant. Edward Mandell House, one of the 21 founders was Woodrow Wilson's chief advisor and from 1913 – 1921, he was rumored to be the nation's real power. Giving money creation powers to bankers the Federal Reserve Act was passed in December of 1913 on his watch, creating the Federal Tax to provide a revenue stream to pay for government debt service and the 16$^{th}$ Amendment was ratified in February. From its beginning the Council on Foreign Relations was committed to a "one world government based on a centralized global financing system". The very principles of this organization make it a somehow "permitted" enemy of the United States government. Ask the U.N., "Why is this tolerated? Explain to us how is this racket is legal"?

It always takes heed to maintain a very elusive and low profile and though sinister in fact, it has thousands of influential members including corporate media. Its membership is 100% American and historian Arthur Schlesinger once called it, "a front organization for the heart of the American Establishment". Publishing only what it wishes the public to know it meets periodically, "privately".

CFR's first cousin the Trilateral Commission, brings together global powerbrokers. Davis Rockefeller founded the TC and is a leading Bilderberger, as well as CFR Chairman Emeritus who continues to finance and support such snake-pit organizations.

(*Reader's note: Ever since childhood, the Rockefellers have been taught to shun and despise "competition". They are as "pro-monopoly" as they come and they live in constant fear of not having enough control.)

The Council on Foreign Relations' power is reflected in their past and current membership, as follows:

- Almost all presidential candidates of both parties

-Leading Senators and Congresspersons

- Key members of the Fourth Estate and their bosses

- Top officials of the Treasury, Judiciary and Commerce departments and leading government agencies, including States; the Defense Department, NSA, CIA and FBI.

Under both Democrats and Republicans the CFR has served as an employment agency for the Federal government. CFR's power and agenda have been unchanged since its founding in 1921, with whoever occupies the White House at its steering wheel. CFR condones and advocates the concept of a global super-state which entails other nations including America, in sacrificing their sovereignty to a centralized power. A former member of Roosevelt's "brain trust", Paul Warburg is CFR's founder. James Warburg his son, told a Senate Foreign Relations Committee in 1950, "We shall have world government whether or not you like it – by conquest or consent". (*Reader's note: It is right about here I would have taken junior to the woodshed for a damn good tail-whacking)

At a Bilderberg Group meeting later in 1992, Henry Kissinger stated, "Today Americans would be outraged if U.N. troops entered Los Angeles to restore order; tomorrow they will be grateful. This is especially true if they were told there was an outside threat from beyond, whether real or promulgated, that threatened our very existence. It is then that all the people of the world will plead with the world leaders to deliver them from this evil – individual rights will be willingly relinquished for the guarantee of their well-being, granted to them by their world government".

(*Reader's note: Sorry to make you soil your diapers Henry, but it ain't going to happen. In studying the history of empires one will always find that once "affluence" arrives on the scene, things start to turn sour and begin the great slide to a fallen society, be it of a nation or a government, regardless of size.

As the reader can plainly see, once human beings reach a certain degree of wealth it is here that things begin to all go wrong for everyone. A feasible concept I've put forth in the past that might intercept both history and a living empire, would be to set "a limit on wealth"; let's say $10 million. Anyone caught trying to supersede or loophole it gets to be shot-at-dawn the following morning. All excess wealth must be put back into the society. I don't know about you, but I'd much rather take my chances with this idea than to live under what Henry and his pack of merry glut-hogs have in store!)

Before 1942 CFR planned a New World Order and a group of CFR members known as the Informal Agenda Group began the United Nations. The original U.N. proposal was drafted by this group. They submitted it to Roosevelt who announced it to the public the very next day. CFR members comprised over 40 of the U.S. delegation at the U.N.'s 1945 founding. Author of "Who Rules America", Professor G. William Domhoff claims that the Council on Foreign Relations operates in, "small groups of about 25 who bring together leaders from the major conspirator categories; industrialists, financiers, ideologues, military, professional specialists, lawyers, medical doctors, organized labor, etc., for detailed discussions of specific topics in the area of foreign affairs."

Domhoff continued, **"The CFR, while not financed by the government,** works so closely with it that it is difficult to distinguish Council action stimulated by government from autonomous actions. It's most important sources of income are leading corporations and major foundations". Just to name three, the Ford Foundation, Carnegie and the Rockefeller Foundations, who are directed by key corporate officials.

The Trilateral Commission's co-founder Zibigniew Brzezinski,

(*Reader's note: You must prepare yourself to read this fellow. He is from another world entirely and is consumed always with the logic that it is "the God given right of a select few, along with their monopolies and trusts, to have you serve them". He's a bit of real fruitcake-piece-of-work-nut-job, so brace yourselves!)

In his book, "Between Two Ages – America's Role in the Technetronic Era" he wrote, "People, governments and economies of all nations must serve the needs of the multinational banks and corporations. The Constitution is inadequate, the old framework of international politics, with their sphere of influence, the fiction of sovereignty, is clearly no longer compatible with reality".

(*Reader's note: No ZB, you're no longer compatible with reality and the only reason the U.S. Constitution might be slightly inadequate is because you and your cronies keep tampering and removing many of its most vital parts which enable it to serve as it was intended. In case you haven't noticed ZB your new world order, childish-make-believe game was concocted over 70 years ago by super wealthy old men who have practically all died off. If anyone's framework is old and outdated it's in your camp. This "new world order" crap is so old there's not a thing "new" about it. As for sovereignty there's nothing factitious about it and if you don't like it you can go back to your low level aristocratic roots in Krakow and stick pins in dolls. I now see its true; you are a "Dr. Evil" hell-bent on destroying the world with nuclear weapons and the reason

Zibigniew Brzezinski

Dr. Evil

Jimmy Carter never had any success in negotiating with the Russians was because of your incalculable degree of hate for them!)

Many entire books have been written on the subjects of various methods, techniques, styles and ideologies in undermining and infiltrating the system to gain boundless wealth.

******************************

(*IMPORTANT Reader's note: Let me attempt to put all of this in a swift perspective. I might have only been 11 years old at the time, but "The Cuban Missile Crisis" of 1962 will always vividly stand out in my mind. What occurred during those two intense weeks in the U.S. was that for 14 days every American felt that this day was their last; that the final nuclear bombs of hell might go off at any moment.

Being in a Roman Catholic School at the time, the Sisters of Charity would line us up two and three times-a-day during emergency drills where we had to quickly get into position in single file along the hallways and have us crouch down in a kneeling position faced up against the walls. It was the most frightening and unusual time of my life.

What is happening now is, as you read this you are actually in a "Cuban Missile Crisis" type event and have been so for every day of almost the past entire year. The paramount and most integral part to this, is that only this time "it is not being reported or discussed" outside the brave Europeans' protests and "it is not trying to be stopped by any government officials"!

What this concludes is that all of the "democratically elected governments" in the entire Western hemisphere are now in a complete disconnect from "their people". Every citizen outside of their governments' is now completely uncoupled from being represented.

This all leads to only one final answer. It is that the entire citizenry in question has now been deserted listlessly in a "pre-prisoner vacuum-in-time", who's voices are now only heard by the very nations to which their governments are positioning themselves to attempt to obliterate, namely Russia and China and the BRICS nations. Western, non-governmental citizens now have more in common with their government's enemies than they do their own government and this is plainly due to the fact that their governments have now delivered them an unspoken message. And it is that their governments now view them as their own enemy too!

It is a bit like the scene from Clint Eastwood's movie "The Outlaw Josie Wales" where in it his Confederate regiment is finally surrendering to the North and turning in their guns. Suddenly, as they are lined-up to take their final oath to the Union of the United States, a Gatling gun is unveiled and all the unarmed prisoners, with the exception of Wales and one young man, are gunned down in cold blood.

So too, it seems true now that the citizenry of the West is being led into a period of pre-slaughter as NATO frantically violates and breaks all treaties in its ushered-in attempts to surround their European compatriots in a strategic, nuclear target zone. Their only salvation lies in the hopes that a new unified front to disband NATO will finally emerge from with the governing bodies. But for every day it does not, the ratio of odds to a complete obliteration of all life becomes more and more likely.)

***************************

One can fill a boxcar with prestigious credentials, millions of dollars, have hundreds of highly influential and prominent associates but when the music stops it all boils down to using conspiracy and illicit means to gain unethical, ultimate wealth and control. There is something very ill about these individuals and it is evident they continue to pass this viral deficiency along in their bloodlines through a genetic malfunction where thoroughbred has eventually turns into inbred.

Take the Rockefellers for example. In “The Rockefeller File” Gary Allen wrote, “By the late nineteenth century the inner sanctums of Wall Street understood that the most efficient way to gain a monopoly was to say it was for the ‘public good and interest’. The one glaring example of the real issue is that not only did John D. Rockefeller teach this to John D. Jr., who taught it to his son David and so on but that ‘they all hated competition’! They hated it with a passion and they relentlessly strove to always eliminate it”.

And therein the entire world can begin to draw a very simple profile of what ‘appears to be’, but ‘is not’, a very complicated matter. Just because one idiot with more money than he knew what

to do with proclaims ‘he must have it all’ and teaches this to his son, who teaches it to his son, does not make it right, acceptable, sane, or anymore justified. It still makes them no more deserving of any rights or privileges than the man who collects the Rockefellers’ garbage.

According to Daniel Estulin, the Bilderberg Group rolled out their desired plans for the global economies. His sources from the last meeting confided that it was divided into two alternatives: "Either a prolonged, agonizing depression which dooms the world to decades of stagnation, decline and poverty, or an intense but shorter depression that paves the way for a new sustainable world order with less sovereignty, but more efficiency". Estulin also noted, "One of the Bilderberg's primary concerns is the danger that **in their zeal to reshape the world by engineering chaos, towards their long-term agenda, could cause the situation to spiral out of control and eventually lead to a scenario where Bilderberg and the global elite in general, become overwhelmed by events and end up losing their control over the plant".**

(*SPECIAL Reader's note: In the event that any of my future critics would attempt to unjustly accuse me of being anti-Semitic, I have racked my brain in coming up with a list of "My Top 56 All-time Heroes" who are, or were either actors, actresses, singers, entertainers, musicians, politicians, government officials, commentators, journalists, or other. Of these fifty-six, 20 have been verified as being of Jewish descent. However, upon further investigation one might actually find, unbeknownst to me, that enough of the remaining 36 non-Jews might in fact also be Jewish, that could easily sway the vote to an even 50%)! They are as follows:

(Kurt Douglas as "Spartacus")

**"<u>My top 56 All-time Heroes & Heroines</u>"**

(Note: an "*" = Jewish)

* Kurt Douglas (actor)

*Rod Steiger (actor)

*Bernie Sanders (politician)

*Bob Newhart (comedian/actor)

(Mitzi Gaynor with "Hollywood's 100 Men")

*Charles Bronson (actor)

*Scarlett Johansson (actress/model)

*Joan Rivers (comedian)

*Bette Midler (singer/dancer/actress/MC/artist)

*Dustin Hoffman (actor)

*Gene Wilder (actor)

*Paul Newman (actor)

*Chico Marx (actor/comedian/musician/singer)

*Groucho Marx (actor/comedian/singer/MC)

*James Caan (actor)

*Paul Newman (actor/businessman/philanthropist)

*Jon Stewart (comedian/commentator/MC)

(Don Rickles at Reagan Inaugural Gala)

*Liza Minelli (singer/dancer/actress/artist)

*Don Rickles (comedian/actor/commentator/MC)

*Steven Seagal (actor/martial arts expert)

*Audrey Hepburn (actress/model)

---

Selena Quintanilla (singer/dancer)

Matt Damon (actor)

Mitzi Gaynor (singer/dancer/actress/MC)

James Coburn (actor)

Lee Marvin (actor)

Dr. Paul-Craig Roberts (politician/writer/commentator/government/economist)

William Cooper (military/writer/MC/reporter)

(Stevie Ray Vaughan)

Carlos Santana (musician/singer)

Phyllis Hyman (singer)

Nina Simone (musician/singer)

Oleta Adams (singer)

Nancy Wilson (singer)

Elmore James (musician/singer)

Joe Satriani (musician/singer)

Stevie Ray Vaughan (musician/singer)

Roy Buchanan (musician)

Ry Cooder (musician/producer/director/choregrapher)

Clint Eastwood (actor/producer/director/choreographer)

James Garner (actor)

(Zhang Ziyi)

Al Pacino (actor)

Henry Fonda (actor)

Kan MiYoun (singer/model/fashion designer)

Zhang Ziyi (actress/model)

Jackie Chan (actor/stuntman/producer/director/choreographer/martial arts expert)

Lucy Lui (actress/model)

Gene Hackman (actor)

Michael Caine (actor)

Patrick McGoohan (actor)

Ben Gazzara (actor)

Robert De Niro (actor)

Natalia Poklonskaya (politician/government/law)

Maria Zakharova (politician/government)

Sergey Lavrov (government/law/speaker/negotiator/politician)

Vladimir Putin (law/politician/government/speaker/martial arts expert/pilot/racecar driver/head of State)

(Henry Fonda in "My Darling Clementine")

Xi Jinping (law/politician/government/speaker/head of State)

Peng Liyuan (military/singer/law/politician/government/fashion designer/speaker/1st Lady)

---

I can't in good faith, gloss over this chapter with a blind eye to an obvious fact. In the realm of the West's quest for global domination and fiscal monopoly, Israel has successfully colonized America. To begin from a poignantly fair and balanced fulcrum, when one tallies the 66 million Russians tortured and put to death by Jews, the magnitude and extent to which their fingers prints have been seen at the scenes of death are most profound. If one were to tally their total amounts of committed genocide including the Canaanites, Palestinians, The Lavon Affair, The USS Liberty Incident, The Kennedy Assassination, The 9-11 Incident, both Iraq Wars, Mali, Libya, Afghanistan, the Ukraine, Syria, numerous false-flag events and add these to the Russian dead, we would get a conservative grand total of 75 million, or a figure in excess of "12 Holocausts". This straight away vaporizes the words of the Israeli writer Ari Shavit who once stated, "We may murder with impunity, because the Holocaust Museum is on our side".

There are good people and bad in every race of people and unfortunately for Jewish people, "ISIS is to the Muslims, what Zionists are to the Jews". The hidden facts surrounding the foundation of Israel is important to consider, if one is to get a better perspective of the situation. Under the tacit understanding that most of them would go and live there, the Jews were given Israel. On their behalf they reneged on their collective promise by their then leaders Theodor Herzel and Chaim Weizmann, as they now prefer to regard Israel as a second home and a place of refuge, should things get too hot for them to handle where they're living at the time.

Herzel himself had once wrote, "Anti-Semitism is an understandable reaction to Jewish defects. I find the anti-Semites are fully within their rights". Let me make one thing very clear, right here and now and that is, this in no way gives anyone the right to condone anti-Semitism! On the understanding of having been given a homeland, in which Jews were obligated to live there, (*Reader's note: I, the writer believes that they should live wherever they wish.) the agreement ended in defeating itself. As Dr. Lasha Darkmoon pointed out, "why is it that 58% of the world's 14 million Jews now live in America, or Europe and only 37% in Israel? It certainly needs to be asked; why were the Palestinians expelled from their own country in order to accommodate another people, who mostly chose to live elsewhere"?

Against this backdrop a large percentage of modern day elites are of the Zionist persuasion and with them came the "weapon" of multiculturalism. Pat Buchanan once stated, "Global elites view the White Western world as the main obstacle standing in the way of a future world government. Multiculturalism is a tool used by the elites to dismantle the Western Civilization". (*Reader's note: It should be mentioned, that Jewish elites do not consider themselves to be white) Multiculturalism is seen by many to be a lethal weapon, not available to the Jews in their past quests over Germany and Russia. It has been concluded by many to have had a devastating effect against America's Euro-American majority. An American dystopia is what can now be noticed, through a darkly lit glass of these traces of gloom. A third world country which may hardly be worth living in for its rapidly diminishing Euro-American majority. In the unipolar sense of the most damaging undermining to democracy, America can likely be credited to the Zionists' monopolarization of the Western news and press media. After all is said and done, I will always know Jews I can admire, respect and hold in high esteem. It is the sins of bad apples whose misdeeds should be exposed.

Israel Shamir once stated, "Palestine is not the ultimate goal of the Jews; the world is. Palestine is just the place for the world State headquarters. The Jews intend to turn Jerusalem into the supreme capital of the world and its rebuilt temple, into the focal point of the Spirit on Earth. Christianity will die, the spirit will depart from the nations in our part of the world and our present, dubious democracy will be supplanted by a vast, theocratic State. De-spiritualized and uprooted, homeless and lonely, yesterday's Masters of the World (WASPs, or White Anglo-Saxon Protestants) will become slaves in all but name. The Jewish universe is good for Jews. It is a curse for others. In the U.S., as Jewish influence has grown steadily since 1968, the lives of ordinary people have worsened. A good time for the Jews is not a good time for mankind. The blessing of the Jews is a curse for others. The regimes that are 'good for Jews' are rarely good for anybody else".

To keep U.S. troops in Afghanistan cost American taxpayers $12 million-an-hour. It was a country America decided to invade through a series of neoconservative lies. Gilad Atzmon commented, "The neocons transformed the American Army into an Israeli mission force". As America's closest ally incredibly, Israel has yet to contribute one single soldier to Washington's wars in Iraq and Afghanistan. In the American fighting forces American Jews are not particularly know to be found in it, nor to be known for their heroism.

Yet far from the din of battle they can be seen most valiantly beating the drums for war the loudest, getting others to fight and die for them while they profit most from the wanton slaughter of innocents. It has been stated by many observers that the days of wine and roses are over for Americans, as its dreams lies dead. And much like Germany and the USSR before it, it is a vanquished, Israeli colony in all but name.

Through various schemes, the serfdom of the West's citizenry seems well underway. Having an ever decreasing hand in the production process of the services and goods being sold to them,

Americans' manufacturing jobs have been offshored out from under them. Another tier to the equation is the financialization of the American economy made noteworthy by Michael Hudson, author of "Killing the Host". This process is in actuality, "a skimming operation" whereby any excess surplus is syphoned off to the financial sector in interest payments while it removes any public presence in the economy.

It is these two schemes which both deprive the citizens of both economic participation and its prosperities, hence the Federal Reserve is "robbing your recovery". What degenerates the Western masses pursuit of happiness even further, is an additional scheme which systematically removes their liberties. This highly corrupt practice recently railroaded the American populace in bullet train fashion, negotiated behind closed doors, not open to the public. Known as the Trans-Pacific Partnerships (TPP), future governance was handed over to corporations and political sovereignty was eliminated. Negotiated in secrecy and having nothing to do with trade, these corporations were granted immunity to the laws of the countries in which they do business in.

Corporate rule replaces American democracy in this most blatantly arrogant violation of racketeering. It contorts the law which enable corporations to sue and fine sovereign governments for any regulations or laws, both existing and prospective, by interpreting their effects on corporate profits, as a "restraint on trade". Hence, the ban on GMOs would be negated under protection of the TPP. In a stark translation, it is a power grab which eliminated representative government. Western unipolar trade agreements are now nothing more than a pocket full of bribed people who supplant law to benefit corporations and supersedes any representative government. This highest form of syndicated crime both eliminates any interference from the public, by placing the defendant (the corporation) above civil law and beyond reproach as it conducts matters in secrecy, but generously lines the pockets of all corrupt parties involved, whose new responsibility is to retool the law for corporate master while still drawing a check from the taxpayer.

Unintended consequences are being predicted to arise from these new “trade partnerships” titled by Western governments. A walking travesty of justice in and of itself, as they insanely demonstrate members of representative forms of government, paid to represent the people of those nations, while accepting additional monies to be non-representatives. It is being predicted that these schemes are running a high risk of attracting revolution and a complete elimination of the 1% then becomes a variable side-effect to these practices. This also bodes the question that in their daring attempts to entice Russia to go to war, Russia may find itself to a front row seat of watching its new adversaries having to go to war with their own people.

Western citizens are being tremendously toyed with by their ruling establishments, by the removal of major keystones to the architecture of their governments, in a fashion which blatantly dares the masses’ composure to protest and the abilities to overthrow their evil robber barons. Unfortunately, the longer the pressure increases the more intense and potentially deadly the likelihood of blow-back, or a complete meltdown to the systems will occur.

As Dr. Paul Craig Roberts, former U.S. Assistant Treasury Secretary, points out, “Once, for example the French people discover they have lost all control of their diet to Monsanto and American Agri-business, the members of the French government that delivered France into dietary bondage to toxic foods, are likely to be killed in the streets”.

The shear practices of unipolarity shares few supporters currently, much beyond a few old psychotic men who concocted it in the name of just a handful like the Rockefellers, who are consumed in psychotic convulsions that are highly prone to monopolistic obsessions and bouts with denial. Globally speaking, 98% of the world prefers peaceful co-existence vs one centralized power of domination, with 1% undecided.

The incomplete power preponderance of the unipole causes anarchy, making unipolarity anarchical. Columbia University's Kenneth Waltz argues that, "A great power cannot exert control everywhere in the world. This in turn affords the relatively weaken countries more freedom to pursue independence from the unipole, who's power projections always remain limited; at least in terms of expansion".

To salvage and restore America would prove to be a tall order. Stacked against it are the elimination of the Glass Stegall Act, Guantanamo still being open, the enactment of the Patriot Act, NSA spying, sizeable portions of the 1st, 4th, 5th, 6th, 8th and 14th Amendments have gone missing, in addition to the enactments of both NAFTA and TPP criminal trading practices. The many errand boys of what few aging maniacs in the rubber rooms atop the pyramid still remain, continue to search and destroy, destabilize and demoralize as privileged white collar criminals, all with some construed form of diplomatic immunity. The lives which they've destroyed shall not go unnoticed and shall not go unanswered for very much longer.

In getting back to the Zionist components in this equation, when one studies all the aspects surrounding the terrorist groups of 2015 like ISIS and the various false-flag events of domestic violence, such as the Paris and California bombings, the identical trademark fingerprints of these crimes and offenses can all be traced directly to one single variety stencil. I call it "The Lavon Affair" stencil. Same M o (Modus operandi) in each and every case and always with high percentages of false attempts to frame and cast suspicion on Muslim people.

(Pinhas Lavon)

Former Israeli Prime Minister Menachem Begin is credited as being "The Father of Terrorism". According to The Hyper Texts, "He once described a massacre as 'a splendid act of conquest'. Albert Einstein and 25 other Jewish intellectuals called Begin and his ilk terrorists, fascists and religious fanatics in a 1948 open letter to the New York Times, comparing them to European fascists like the Nazi. Begin killed Brits, Arabs and Jews with reckless abandon, including civilians and was involved in the Deir Yassin Massacre and other acts of terrorism such as the bombing of the King David Hotel".

THE FATHER OF TERRORISM
"How does it feel, in the light of all that's going on, to be the father of terrorism in the Middle East?"
"In the Middle East?" he [Begin] bellowed, in his thick, cartoon accent. "In all the world!"
- Menachem Begin to Russell Warren Howe, January 1974

(King David Hotel, before & after 1946)

Louisiana.

SINGLE COPY 5 CENTS

Entered N. O. Postoffice as Second-Class Matter Under Act of March 3, 1879

# HOTEL BLAST KILLS 93 IN JERUSALEM

M'CAIN ATTEMPTS TO QUALIFY, FAILS

14 British Officers Victims of Bomb Planted by 'Jewish Terrorists'

(The Associated Press)

Jerusalem, July 22.—The Palestine government an-

In the early 1950's, "The Lavon Affair" was a very covert and secret Israeli mission of premeditated terrorism that began to take shape under the code name, "Operation Susannah". It was a failed false-flag operation, both very secretive in planning and very Israeli in its origin and was to be carried out in Egypt during the summer of 1954. Recruited by Israeli Intelligence a group of Egyptian Jews were to plant bombs in American educational centers, libraries and American and British-owned civilian targets. The detonators were timed to set the bombs off, several hours after closing time.

(Suez Canal early 1950's)

The attacks, with the aim of creating a climate of sufficient violence and instability, were to be blamed on the Muslim Brotherhood, Egyptian Communists, unspecified malcontents and locals, to induce the British government to retain its occupying forces in the Suez Canal zone. The operation caused no casualties, except for when a bomb carried by operative Philip Nathanson, went off prematurely in his pocket within a movie theater. There were also two suicides committed by cell operatives after capture and two other operatives in Egypt were tried, convicted and executed.

Ultimately the operation became known as "The Lavon Affair" after Pinhas Lavon, the then Israeli Defense Minister, who as a consequence of the incident, was forced to resign. In Israel it was euphemistically referred to as the "Unfortunate Affair", or "The Bad Business", just before Lavon's resignation. For 51 years Israel denied any involvement, until 2005 when Israeli President Moshe Katzav awarded certificates of appreciation to the surviving agents, who were officially honored.

The United States had initiated a more activist policy in support of Egyptian nationalism, early in the 1950's. The regional hegemony of Britain was cast into contrast, due to its policies. American policy having eventually encouraged Britain to withdraw troops, infuriated Israel's fear that it might embolden Egyptian President's Nasser to seek military ambitions against them. After a meek attempt by Israel to influence this policy by diplomatic means, it gave up in frustration.

The chief of Israel's military intelligence Aman, Colonel Binyamin Gibli, initiated "Operation Susannah during the summer of 1954, in order to reverse that decision. The objective was to

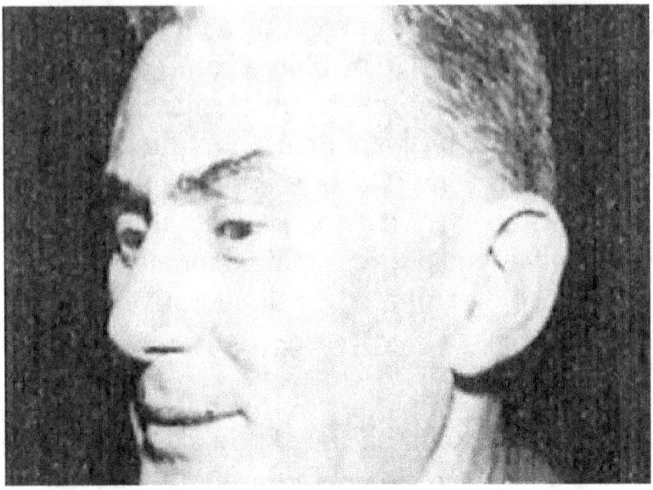

(Col. Binyamin Gibli)

create an atmosphere in which the British and American opponents of the British withdrawal would gain an upper hand and block this withdrawal through bombings and other acts of "terrorism" and destabilization (*Readers note: Does this sound familiar?). This was to be carried out, while at the same time concealing any Israeli involvement. Suspicion would be orchestrated to fall on the Muslim Brotherhood, Communists and others and avoiding detection was strongly urged on the team.

Unit 131 the top secret cell, had been under Aman, Israel's military intelligence since 1950, but under the Mossad, Israel's national intelligence since 1948 and was responsible for carrying out the operations. Unit 131 was a bitter dispute between Aman and the Mossad, over which agency should control Operation Susannah at the time. Several years before, Israeli intelligence officer Avram Dar, undercover as a British citizen named John Darling from Gibraltar, arrived in Cairo and recruited Unit 131 operatives. Dar recruited several Egyptian Jews, previously involved in illegal emigration activities and trained them for more precise, covert operations.

During the spring of 1954, the Aman decided to activate the network. In Alexandria on July 2, the cell detonated bombs at a post office. In Cairo, on July 14, it bombed a British owned theatre and the libraries of the U.S. Information Agency. Consisting of bags of acid placed over nitroglycerine, the homemade bombs were inserted in books and then placed back on the shelves of the library, just before closing. As the acid ate through the bags several hours later, the bombs would explode.

Israeli agent Avri Elad (Avraham Seidenwerg) was sent to oversee the operation before the group began. Assuming the identity of Paul Frank, a former SS officer with Nazi underground connections. But Egyptian intelligence was tipped off by Avri, who decided to take the roll as a double agent. The Egyptians followed a suspect to his target and with a firetruck standing by, outside the Rio Theatre. When the operative Philip Nathanson's bomb exploded prematurely in his pocket, Egyptian authorities arrested what remained of him. They later found incriminating evidence after searching his apartment, including a list of names of his accomplices.

Undercover Israelis and several Egyptian Jewish suspects were arrested. Managing to escape was Col. Dar and Elad, while two other suspects, Meir Max Bineth and Yosef Carmon committed suicide in prison. The Egyptian trial ran from December 11$^{th}$ to January 27$^{th}$, 1955. Two were acquitted, two were condemned to execution by hanging and the remaining suspects all received lengthy sentences.

Both publicized and criticized as a show trial back in Israel, its military censored the press and the Israeli public was kept in the dark. The Lavon Affair and Operation Susannah, turned out to be disastrous for Israel. Considerable political turmoil ensued in the incident's aftermath for some time. Israel's relationships with Britain and the U.S. were greatly damaged for many years.

What remains both paramount and perplexing for researchers to this day is the incredibly different manner Israel was treated, in its aftermath of its attack on the USS Liberty, (The USS Liberty Incident) where U.S. personnel were openly murdered at sea.

The New World Order "is" a Lavon Affair because the New World Order "is terrorism"; in its funding and support of State sponsored terrorism, in its malicious physical sense of destroying the life and limb of its innocent bystanders being murder as collateral damage, either directly or in its many false-flag events. To further explain and describe, in its financial policies, in its government policies, in its domestic policies, in its use of torture (Guantanamo being living proof), violations of human rights, international law and its shear agenda!

The Bilderberg Group cannot be made an exception here, as it too practices many forms of monopolistic terrorism with its various Rockefellian methods and impositions to its financial and trade agendas. "World domination" and "Centralized control" are the things of dinosaur-minded men who are detached from reality and any compassion for humanity outside their own voracious appetites for "more"!

Jewish terrorists have blown the Mason's masonry right out of the apex. That is why it is time for "new BRICS" and that is why it is time for every race and persuasion of people in the world today to reach across the aisles and join together in the permanent eradication of Zionism, a Zionist police State and/or a New World Order because they are all one in the same and they are all anti-people, anti-culture, anti-family, anti-heritage, anti-religious, sacrilegious, anti-sovereignty, anti-moral, anti-ethical, anti-just, anti-competitive, anti-diversity, anti-choice, anti-peace and anti-human rights, freedom and democracy!

It is time for every Japanese and Chinese to drop their differences in this instance, just as it is time for every Muslim and

Jew. Though it rarely gets any press coverage, in places like Russia and Iran Jews and Muslims have been peacefully co-existing alongside one another for decades! It is the agenda of the ole-fashioned Menachem Begin mind-set being implemented by tyrannical madmen such as Benjamin Netanyahu who falsely polarize this peace through direct and premeditated campaigns of agitation under false pretense, fueling the venomous fires and froth under the West's Zionist presstitude press! Therefore, it is also time for every authentic Muslim and Jew to voice objection and to distance themselves from the extremists within their own ranks who are though miniscule in number, they are counterfeit in their genuine beliefs and are being unjustly rewarded the majority of global press coverage!

I have taught thousands of the "next" new, upcoming generation and I can attest here and now that they have no interests whatsoever in living in a world which is nothing more than one, giant, global North Korea. And this my friend, is all the New World Order really is.

# Chapter XIII

## Making Good Mortar

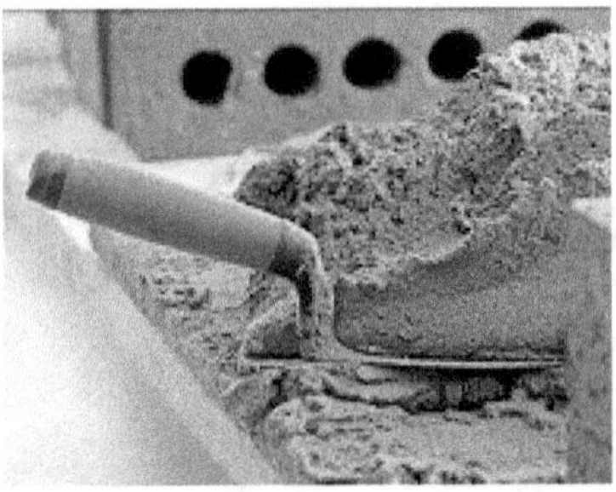

On the second to the last day of 2015 Chinese President Xi Jinping and Vladimir Putin vowed to boost the "strategic partnership" as they exchanged New Year's greetings. President Xi in his message said, "The China-Russia comprehensive strategic partnership of coordination was maintained at a high level in 2015". He also praised the proposed integration of China's ambitious Silk Road Economic Belt, with that of the Russia-led Eurasian Economic Union. The two allies also cooperated closely on international affairs, Xi said.

President Xi also mentioned high-level Sino-Russian ties have, "injected positive energy into the construction of a new-type of international relations, featuring cooperation and win-win situations". China and Russia signed more than 30 cooperation documents in energy, investments, financing, high-technology and other areas, the month prior during the China visit of Russian Premier Dmitry Medvedev. Energy giants Sinopec and Rosneft signed a MOU (memorandum of understanding) on oil and gas projects in eastern Siberia, while CNPC and Gazprom inked an agreement on the design and construction of the cross-border section of China-Russia east-route natural gas pipeline.

Russia's State corporation, Vnesheconombank (VEB) and the China Development Bank, also signed an agreement on a $10 billion yuan ($1.56 billion) loan. In addition, this past December, 2015 the central banks of the two countries signed an agreement to promote local currency settlements, bank card issuance, access to local-currency bond markets and credit rating partnerships.

Putin meanwhile, in his speech to Xi on the New Year, as well as during the Chinese Spring Festival, noted that, "The outgoing year has seen a number of significant developments in relations between Russia and China. Thus, the joint celebrations of the 70th anniversary of Victory in WW II, helped strengthen the traditional Russian-Chinese friendship", said a Kremlin statement. Putin also stressed that he is looking forward to further consecutive work to develop the entire range of Russian-Chinese ties. Russia and China have set a bilateral trade target of $200 billion by 2020.

Accounting for 11.3% of Russia's foreign trade in 2014, China is Russia's biggest foreign trade partner. With a share of 2.2% in China's foreign trade of the same period, Russia is China's 9th trade partner in size. Owing to the economic downturn in Russia and China's slowdown, bilateral-trade has dropped for 2015. Russian imports from China stood at $22.4 Billion, down from 32.7%, while Russia's exports to China were $19.1 billion, or down 26%.

However, continuing unabated were Chinese investment into the Russia economy, which reached $9.7 billion as of June, 2015, up 11.9%.China's top oil supplier has been taken over by Russia during 2015 and in the first six months, Russia's oil exports to China increased 15%, compared with the previous year.

In a very wise, yet surprising move, the government of the Philippines announced it has joined the China-led Asia Infrastructure Investment Bank, just days after it was formally launched and despite pressures from the United States, who was against the idea. The Philippines is technically a U.S. ally in the region, but as with Japan, it remains to be seen just how extensive and loyal this relationship will become, given China's economic rise and the U.S. now both a destitute and unipolar nation. Japan too, though receiving pressure from the U.S. discouraging economic relations with the multipolar nations, has ignored those warnings and is growing closer with both China and Russia, in terms of international trade, business and finance. Japan, the U.S. and EU are now the most overextended nation bloc's globally and are gravely at risk. In the case of Japan, this is due to poor management and in the case of the U.S. and EU, the unipolar component in their extraordinarily high percentages in defense spending and military upkeep. The economies of the U.S. and EU are slated to burst-and-crash, shortly following the 2016 U.S. elections.

The Philippines Department of Finance (DOF) in Manila stated, "The Republic of the Philippines will be signing the Articles of Agreement (AOA) of the Asia Infrastructure Investment Bank, joining the newly created multilateral institution aimed at boosting infrastructure development and connectivity". The Philippines announcement came two days before the deadline for prospective founding members to sign the AIIB. Half of the EU, all of the Asian bloc ASEAN and the entire BRICS coalition comprise its founding members. The U.S. on the other hand, seems to carelessly subject itself into a deeper sense of isolationism, in an embarrassing global demonstration of pigheadedness, denial, loose-cannon diplomacy and destructive lawlessness and treaty-breaking. Obviously those Lavon Affair-type terrorists are still in command of its steering.

In parts of the South China Sea, the Philippines has a dispute with China over territorial claims. However, Philippine Benigno Aquino smiled and shook hands with China President Xi during the APEC summit in Beijing of 2014. The two are said to have had respectful, informal conversation. The Philippines has taken its case to the Permanent Court of Arbitration in the Hague, but China has declined to take part. Philippines Vice President Jejomar Ninay has said he wants the country to be a member of the China-backed bank because it will spur more domestic investment and employment in his country. Observers will be waiting to see if that statement comes "corruption-free". A government statement said the country's indicative, paid-in-capital will be $196 million, payable in 5 years, or $39 million per annum.

The AIIB's Board of Directors and Executive Council had their first meeting January 16 – 18, 2016 at its headquarters in Beijing. The bank now has 57 members which include Germany, France, Italy and the U.K. Financing infrastructure development across Asia, is the task of the China-backed bank multilateral development institution. The AIIB will finance infrastructure projects like the construction of roads, railways and airports in the Asia-Pacific Region, with an authorized capital of $100 billion.

To maintain the current economic growth rates the Asia Development Bank (ADB) has estimated that during the next decade Asian countries will need $8 trillion in infrastructure investments. Extending China's financial reach, the AIIB will compete not only with the World Bank, but also with the Asia Development Bank, which is heavily dominated by Japan.

There's much more happening in the mortar than meets the eye. The first day of 2016 marked the start of Russia's sanctions against Ukraine and Turkey. (*Reader's note: Financial and geopolitical gurus, pundits and experts, from Gerald Celente to Dr. Paul-Craig Roberts and from Max Keiser to Harry Dent have often been sounding the alarms in their concerns of the following deja'vu: first comes currency wars, then trade wars, followed by a real war!) Adopted by Moscow, the measures are in rebuttal to Turkey's downing of a Russian Su-24 in November of 2015. Russia is halting the imports of a wide range of agricultural products, according to a decree signed by President Putin on November 28, 2015. The products include fruits, vegetables, salt, poultry products and more.

The visa-free travel regime once enjoyed between the two countries has also been suspended to, "ensure the national security of the Russian Federation from criminal and other illegal activities", while its charter flights in both directions have now been banned. Turkey's previous annual agricultural exports to Russia amounted to more than $1 billion. The Ukraine likewise will also see severe cutbacks, as many new restrictive regulations in 2016 get underway.

During June of 2015 saw India's eminent banker K.V. Kamath, take over as the first president of the BRICS $100 billion New Development Bank. The 67 year old Kamath is the non-executive Chairman of India's largest, private sector bank ICIC and is also the non-executive Chairman of IT bellwether Infosys. Headquartered in Shanghai, the New Development Bank as per agreement, granted India the rights to nominate its first president. The BRICS nations currently account for nearly $16 trillion in GDP and 40% of the world's population. India is hoping to receive more funds for infrastructure development from the bank. To ensure that the development bank does not fall into the ownership pattern of the IMF (International Monetary Fund) and World Bank, an equal capital contribution method will be used, without distorted shareholding.

Other interesting developments adding cohesive strength to the BRICS mortar will be its next G-20 meeting in Hangzhou, China

(September, 2016). China President Xi Jinping announced its theme of "promoting the innovative, dynamic, concerted and inclusive world economy". This dovetails with the G-20's lasting efforts in promoting global innovative growth, perfecting economic and financial governance and stimulating international trade and investment in order to achieve an inclusive and concerted development.

It is this word "inclusive" which represents the entire, contrasting differences between the multipolar and unipolar worlds. For here we find ourselves sitting on the outskirts of the West's privileged atrocities and genocide of scorched battlefields where within you will find hundreds upon hundreds of thousands of defenseless and senseless murdered victims' bodies strewn over thousands of square hectares of devastated civilizations, who once thrived with vitality and now lie in ruins. This all coming to pass because a handful of "exclusive" and affluent few of the West cannot find it in themselves to share and coexist. It is for this and them alone that each one of us are being forced to live on the brink of total annihilation and the destruction of all life.

The insiders to this Hangzhou, China G-20 Summit will tell you that the shortened version to its theme will actually boil down to this: that the time has arrived where "the G-20 must act, in order for it to prevent itself from becoming a mere talk-shop"! The G-20 has arrived at an historic juncture of transforming itself from a "fire brigade" into "a mechanism for actual change" in addressing the structural deficiencies in the world economy, as China assumes the chairmanship. In shepherding the G-20 and the world economy in the best direction, naturally greater expectations have risen to the surface for China. The G-20 must now ask itself what are the most important expectations and for China to meet them, what should be done? In a broad sense there are three basic reasons why China has identified its theme:

1) The economic recovery is slow: With unsatisfactory growth and no visible driving force, even though the world economy is more or less out of the financial crisis, the pulse of its growth is lackluster. I would conjecture this is due to the fact that until the G-20 completely uncouples from the West, a world where lop-sided amounts of revenues are wasted on defense and interest payments, it will continue to feel its undertow. It would only make good fiscal sense to phase-out any reliance's on Western currencies, Wall Street derivatives and exports. The world economy is currently being forced to split away from a Western contagion of "war based" and "deficit based" economics. The unipolar model currently in operation is completely Hitleresque. Hitler never had a "plan for a peace-time economy", ever. His Dr. Strangelove mindset, much like the current Rothschild's, Soros's, Rockefeller's and Warburg's, was completely based on always being in "a perpetual state of war".

The up and coming generation will see to it that these practices of yesterday's fossilized heroes, gets a quick ultimatum. In the approaching future, the West's own "Generation Z", will insist upon their older generations to play multipolar ball, or it will sentence them to eat cake!

2) A need for active reforms: With trade now being a bit messy and confusing, reforms in global governance and international rules-making need to be formatted and swiftly put into practice.

3) Desires for innovation, greenness and a willingness to share: It has become evident that in coordinating global macro-economic policies, the G-20 feels a sense of being powerless and a bit frustrated.

For the 2016-2020 period, China wishes to develop an innovative, coordinated, much greener, open and sharing economy, which matches the Hangzhou Summit's theme. As set by its Brisbane Summit of 2014, G-20 members are presently engaged in meeting the target of an additional 2% GDP growth by 2018. If one makes a unipolar comparison here, NATO's demanding countries like Italy to spend 2% of their GDP on "weapons" is completely idiotic. As mentioned previously, this correlates into Italy spending $100 million-a-day on this, which is a global economic atrocity in and of itself. It makes no small wonder out of why nations are distancing themselves from the fossilized controllers of yesterday's leading Western nations.

The G-20 nations must navigate towards their objectives while juggling the demands of climate change, increased terrorist attacks, the effects of affluence on the middle class and keeping abreast of the geopolitical hot-spots. Half of these issues are being caused by the wakes created from the unipolar worlds' desperate, highly reckless, volatile and extremely "nuclear flammable" attempts of trying to achieve "World War III"! This broadcasts interference for those trying to conduct an economy in countries which mind their own business peacefully.

China has now arrived at the moment to lead global governance. This will require it to reform its architecture. The first thing the BRICS's G-20 members must change is "their gullibility" and to stop accepting anything the West, the IMF, the World Bank, or the WTO has to say, at face value. It must decide and tell them what they themselves will need to do. Any Japan-US-EU figures for GDP and unemployment will no longer be globally accepted or believed, in light of the West's over exposure to the illicit practices of its sole economics professor, the Wharton School of "cooked book" Economics". At this writing the U.S. unemployment rate is somewhere between 17.7 to 23%. And yet it will insist it is only 5.7% once the rate is ran through the Wharton's Rube Goldberg-smoke-and-mirrors sawmill of economic delusion. The West, through its numerous antics of being caught shooting itself in the foot, has made itself a laughing stock globally, being perceived as only a predictable has-been superpower, destitute and narrow-minded, who's only claim to fame is as a Jon Lovitz's character as the president of pathological liars anonymous. The U.S. dollar is not strong, it is worthless. The EU is not solvent, it is on the brink of collapse and Japan has not had an economy since 1985.

The "Washington Consensus" is no longer relevant and needs to be removed from the global equation of governance in trade and the economic system. It is an outdated, highly corrupt and failed corporatocracy stolen from the old Soviet Union. It has more holes to fill than the existing body which remains. For the next 50 years the unipolar world will rely on the BRICS G-20, far more than the other way around, if it is to survive at all. This demands the West will have to take a numbered ticket and wait in line, just like everybody else. It has nothing remaining to respect and it has worn out its welcome.

For the G-20 Summit in Hangzhou to achieve success will depend on China "walking the walk". Bearing testimony to this reality are the world trade figures with annual growth rates slowing from 2008's 7% to the present 3%. The culprits to the global economic problem are systemic and structural. They need to be swiftly renovated and converted over to a more modern framework. One that has a new future in mind and is geared to the Hangzhou Summit's theme, through a G-20 perspective and not of old, antiquated and pre-Warsaw pact conscientiousness. The West still hasn't gotten it through its thick, Neanderthal cranium yet, that it is no longer the boss of bosses, but it will eventually have no other choice. The West is trying to play road-hog on a four lane highway with a Willys Jeep. This whole transformation, once Generation –Z has hog-tied the elitist fossils and hauled them off to the wax museum, will entail its share of sweet pain and tough love. Teaching the West how to become "an equal team player" will be a lot like teaching the Royal Family how to live on $2,500-a-month.

China needs to get addressing issues such as commodity prices which are being artificially exacerbated lower by the subsidies of Western governments who are printing money which is backed by nothing but the paper it was printed on. Again, this is being orchestrated by those "Lavon Affair terrorists" who are still using the antique USSR corporatocracy models of economics. This is being used in their attempts to destroy the small farmers as mentioned in the Chapter on Modi. In short, the BRICS G-20 members will have to deliver the West a strict order of discipline, with ultimatums and real threats to cut the West out-of-the-picture.

There's nothing wrong with the BRICS G-20's economic agenda, so long as they will act to design them to be much less affected by Western hegemony. Being known for their Zionist created false-flags, the West needs to be told "publicly" to not even think about it, when it comes to addressing terrorist possibilities in the future. The West has made its bed and it now needs it shoved back into its face, so the world will become more confident to it more accountable.

The West is riding on a pre-60's reputation which is nothing more than a magician's illusion. It is like a once wealthy patron of a prestigious country club who has suddenly lost all his riches, yet still comes into the clubhouse as if nothing has changed. He proceeds to order a big dinner and buy a round of drinks for all his friends and on his way out the door he hollers, "Put it on my tab Charlie"! The West has become too assuming in more and more matters it has no business being involved in, often showing up uninvited as "the jerk" who wouldn't leave the party, long after it had ended.

The G-20 Summit for 2016 will demand "actions" and commitments to implementation, not just rhetoric. Their discussions will require "teeth" and a demonstration by its ministers will now commit to executing their list of themes, beyond the feel-good, warm and fuzzy stages. Participation of business leaders in the G-20 Summit is essential and it would serve them well to proceed as early as possible for those preparations. Ex-China members need to "show-and-tell" and commit to doing what plans they have for being far less reliant on resource exports in the immediate future. A prominent strategy from the minute China is let out of the gate at the Summit's onset, should be to swiftly block Turkey, the EU and US from hijacking the Summit's driving intentions and that is collaborating "legitimate" trade. Any attempts to turning the Summit into a crying session for their Syrian blowback should be promptly dismissed as "off topic".

The Israeli-U.S. colony was recently exposed chauffeuring around ISIS troops. The Turkish president and his son have been caught having their hands in the same cookie jar as ISIS and we already know that the European governors grow no balls. So in addressing any "terrorist issues" at this Summit requires quickly dumping the blame on the true instigators, discount the topic as "a Western problem" and promptly move on to the economic matters at hand. As evidenced by the following, there's too much on the plate at stake to permit it to be derailed by bad actors and Turkish-Zionist shenanigans. Their list of themes will always include macroeconomics, labor, aging, another "Western" problem known as corruption, energy, infrastructure, financial architecture, health, investments, banking, taxes, sustainability and regulations.

What the Western presstitude press and its university professors are completely missing in point, are the issues attached to the Hangzhou Summit which can be summed up in three aspects:

1) The world no longer recognizes a "Washington Consensus".

2) When Turkey and Israel's U.S. colony have been openly exposed to violating treaties, international law, human rights, laws related to terrorism by aiding and abetting terrorists, collusion laws by supporting the sale and transport of stolen oil and illicit narcotics, don't come to the table with a gun half-cocked unless you're prepared to use it and this would include not permitted all these offenses to go discounted as non-events.

3) The Brookings Crime Institute, the Wharton School of Cooked-book Economics and the Pew Propaganda Pollsters are also no longer recognized outside the West. How Pew can turn a Vladimir Putin 65% approval rating into 20% is the same way Wharton converts a 17.5% unemployment rate into 5.7%.Brooking might still get away with telling U.S. presidents what to do, but the buck stops at the International Dateline.

So if even the mention of "terrorism" comes up at the 2016 G-20 Summit by "any" Western entity, they should be asked to first answer why it has just been recently unearthed by Russian, Turkish, European and American officials with supporting evidence, that Turkey's President Erdogan has been recruiting and supporting ISIS. It has been discovered further that his son Bilal Erdogan has been using his oil tankers to transport "ISIS" stolen Iraqi and Syrian oil while his sister Sumeyye Erdogan provides us with the icing on the cake, being exposed running a secret hospital camp, just across the Syrian border in Turkey where she helps patches-up ISIS members for reentry back into terrorizing.

According to French geopolitical analyst, Thierry Meyssan, Turkey's President Erdogan organized the pillage of Syria, dismantling all factories in Aleppo by stealing machine tools and organizing archeological thefts and sales of treasuries. The Turkish president, along with General Benoit Puga, Chief of Staff for the Elysee' (France's presidential headquarters), organized the chemical bombing of Damascus in August of 2013, according to Meyssan. We are talking about "a NATO member nation here"!

This in and of itself proves more than ample ammo to deflect any terrorist issues which might arise from the West, so that China's President Xi can openly discuss his themes, intentions and plans for implementation of a more decent world.

# Chapter XIV

## West's Facebook Mind-control

Social Observers and experts alike are becoming increasingly concerned over the many negative aspects now associated with Facebook. As with anything online today, when dealing with a cyber digital community it immediately becomes difficult to assess, as we are not dealing with a true realm here, but rather an imagery-sensory experience where you are willing to subject yourself to a form of machine generated sight and sound symmetry to which you have no control over, other than to switch to another channel line or shut it off.

For one to completely decipher, detect, or determine whether or not something else is actually occurring simultaneously during your experience cannot be performed by the average lay person. One would need a panel of psychologists, technicians and NSA and/or CIA specialists to monitor your time spent during your online experience, to truly confirm if you're being harmfully manipulated or subliminally approached or not. Since I confess I am not privy to such luxuries, or even to having any type of security clearance, I can only attempt to interpret notes, articles, books, messages and the loudest roars coming from the herds' trending experiences.

One thing that's for certain from the beginning is that it is true Facebook does collect and store your personal data and preferences to form a profile which it uses to target users. I used to pass the Facebook headquarters in Menlo Park on almost a daily basis while I was a technician for Pentair. Facebook purchased (or leased) the original waterfront (San Francisco Bay) campus from Sun Microsystems. They then purchased an additional 60 acres across the street and began new construction, in close proximity to the Stanford Research Institute (SRI), which ironically was made famous for performing the MK Ultra "mind-control" experiments affiliated with the Tavistock Institute of Human Relations and the CIA, but that's another can of worms entirely (or is it?). I recall seeing scores of trailer loads of soil which were being hauled offsite during this Facebook construction and after investigating I was told some of the soil had contained PCBs. I thought that to be a bit peculiar since the whole site lays smack alongside the pristine wetlands of the Don Edwards National Wildlife Refuge. I later discovered that biological warfare munitions were also stored and used there once for some experiments in this region and in association with SRI and the Department of Defense (DOD).

It was very funny I thought that here, in a one square mile space you have Facebook and SRI sitting alongside a pristine wildlife wetlands just off the Dumbarton Bridge, where PCBs were once permitted to flourish while SRI was involved with biological weapons and mind-control experiments. So in the future I wouldn't allow yourself to be snookered into believing that the entities located on this "glowing" piece of property are in anyway ethical or environmentally friendly! However I can't fully put the blame on SRI as its former neighbor was also once a Pentair affiliate known as Raychem and I have no idea what those people were up to. By the way, PCBs are a human carcinogen which greatly increases the susceptibility to all major diseases, including heart disease and diabetes. Just some food for thought if you happen to be one of those health conscious joggers or cyclists who frequent the vicinity of this darling Facebook campus. If you're ever there, perhaps you might like to inquire to the local management if they also removed all the local fish who might of ever been exposed to these past disgraces, now that they've successfully corrected the mysterious "brain disease" which once afflicted the local white pelican population!

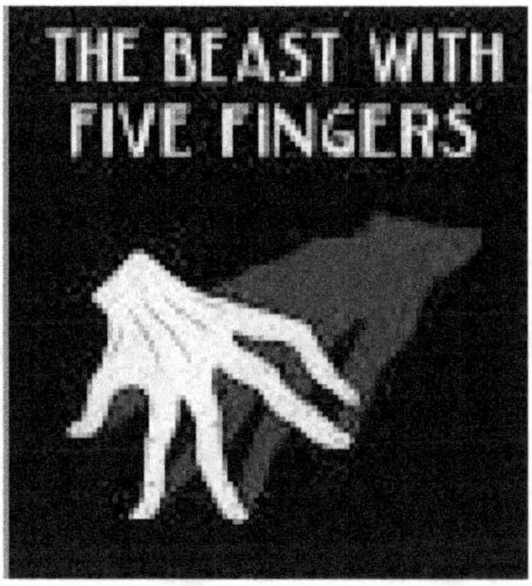


Getting back to the matters of “The Hand”, it is common knowledge that Facebook now not only collects your data, but also your online search data. Once this occurs, the user has just surrendered their mind to an invisible monitoring system which stores every detail of your actions, thoughts and general disposition. Data security expert Bruce Schneier comments that data-brokers, “collect demographic information, names, addresses, telephone numbers, e-mail addresses, gender, age, marital status, the presence of children in household and their number and ages, education level, profession, income level, political affiliations, cars driven, and information concerning homes and other property. They collect lists of things you’ve purchased, how much you paid for them and where. They keep track of deaths in the family, divorces, and diseases in your family. They also collect log of all the places you’ve visited while on the internet. So it would be safe to say that if you have a Facebook account, every time you go online it is like driving in your car with a constant spy sitting in the back seat. The irony in all this monitoring is that it can also be a complete waste of time, money and resources for these companies. Take myself for instance, who often has researched daily as many different sources related to geopolitical and economic events as possible; say from 40 different news sources globally, in order to have my news blog-site constantly updated for the leading stories related to this subject matter. Drawing a conclusion as to what type of individual is at the wheel of my keyboard would obviously reap a constant, completely inaccurate profile of me. Another case in point is the 250 lb. uncle who decides to buy his twinkle toe niece a pair of ballet slippers online and then proceeds to get targeted for months afterwards with annoying ads for clothing pegged to a petite junior miss.

What seems to make Facebook a bit more venomous is it deliberately hides the extent of its datamining and has also been seen in bed with the U.S. Department of Defense and the CIA. It has been determined that Facebook now collects more information on its member users than the NSA, while making vast sums of money in the process. Young unsuspecting users will never possess, experience or know "true privacy" ever, in any way, shape, or form for their entire lives. They have been "permanently tagged", strip-searched and tattooed, while their brains have already been tenderized, exposing them to the vulnerabilities of any array of mind-control their Facebook handlers may choose to utilize on any given day.

This once fun, harmless and useful tool seems to have transformed into an intrusive, tracking monster beyond any Orwellian comprehension. There's also side-effects now being reported as well, from researchers whose subjects have complained of bouts with depression, anxiety, malcontent, sensations of emptiness, headaches, nausea, envy and even anger. A new statistic reports that 50% of all American divorces involved some form of cause connected to Facebook.

At Berlin's Humbolt University, researcher Hanna Krasnova from the Institute of Information Systems shared, "We were surprised by how many people have a negative experience from Facebook, with envy leaving them feeling lonely, frustrated or angry. From our observations, some of these people will leave Facebook, or at least reduce their use of it".

Author David Rainshek contends that Facebook's danger is its "mind altering" abilities: "Absolutely, it significantly changes the physical structure of your brain's neural network, which even changes how you feel about yourself and other people". He also cites evidence that, "Facebook use can alter, or upset the amounts of dopamine coming from a neurotransmitter within the brain".

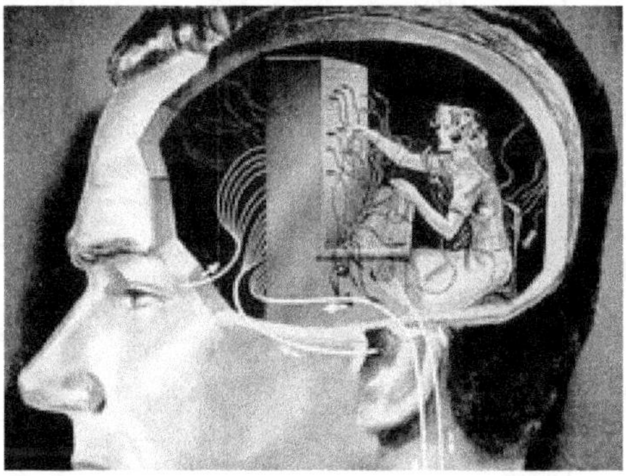

Anonymous claims Facebook is nothing more than co-intel-pro with slick packaging. Part of a new breed of spy networks designed to profile-and-target and eventually control the mind, given its close proximity to SRI, its seamless access to the Tavistock Institute and its cultivated relationships with both the Department of Defense and the CIA.

**It turns out that one of the researchers who ran Facebook's recent psychological experiments received funding from the U.S. Department of Defense to study the contagion of ideas**

In what appears to be a clear cut case of the devil in sheep's clothing, Facebook carefully spins a likeable layer of user-friendly, digital home-Mom wrapper around a black foray of psycho-profiling, emotional-undermining and mind-handling. This all is performed for instant profits from the marketing of lost souls, without their permission or knowledge, for a cryptocracy who wishes to know every detail of your life, while tracking your every location at every moment.

From the CIA's favorite breeding grounds of Harvard University, 3 of its students founded Facebook. Their first seed money came in the form of a $500,000 check from Peter Thiel, founder and former CEO of Paypal. Thiel is a graduate of the home to CIA mind-control projects such as MK Ultra and NSA computer research, Stanford University. Being a former columnist for the Wall Street Journal, he is an avowed neocon and globalist, making him a devout supporter of the New World Order flank. His book, "The Diversity Myth" received praises from none other than the founder of the Project for a New American Century (PNAC), William Kristol who replaced this former think tank which aided "The 9-11 Incident" with the Foreign Policy Initiative. His book also received praises from Christopher Cox, Edward Meese and Linda Chavez, also NWO gnomes. Thiel, who personally donated money to Arnold Schwarzenegger's campaign, sits on the Board of Directors of the radical right-wing Vanguard PAC.

Evidently the shadowy world of black ops doesn't stop here for Facebook. Well before Mark Zuckerberg rose to the helm, Facebook received $13 million in venture capital backing from Accel Partners. The manager of Accel, James Breyer, was then on the Board of Directors of National Ventures Capital Association (NVCA), with Gilman Louie, the then head of In-Q-Tel. In 1999 the CIA set up In-Q-Tel with an agenda of fostering companies that provided "data warehousing and mining", as their goal. "Profiling search agents" who were "self-sustaining" were also its goals. Sure sounds like "The Hand" (Facebook) to me.

(Peter Lorre in "The Beast With Five Fingers" 1946)

With a program so innocuous in appearance, it now serves as the best way to spy on possible radicals and student activists. As you can see for yourself, Facebook already allows for easy government profiling as it categorizes its users on the scale of "Very Liberal' to "Very Conservative". Facebook currently categorizes "thought crimes" as it tracks and stores any users who have hit the wrong keys, in their eyes, such as words like "New World Order", "anarchist" and "protest", just to list a few.

When AOL admitted to handing over emails and web logs to the FBI and NSA, they revealed a new privacy policy. It basically stated, “You waive all and any right to privacy”. Immediately, users were warned by civil liberties advocates that the all-seeing Illuminati eye logo’s company could record all their communications. But with so much MTV to watch at the time and gang’sta rap to emulate, it appears very few of them ever listened.

The CIA then announced it would be hiring students to spy on campus activists. This clearly is quite an obvious and blatant sign that the CIA of today has been completely taken over from within, by a highly illegal and elite group of people who are now in and of themselves, “enemies-of-the-State”; the authentic United States. This lends evidence to the theory which believes that if America is ever defeated and falls it will be “an implosive event” caused from within and not an outside force.

Information like the kind these so-called CIA student-recruits were to be obtaining, can be stored in penta-byte databases linked to a micro-chipped, National ID card. Some critics chide that Facebook must first weed out the student troublemakers (anyone who questions), before they can solder Brain Gate chips in our brains, or implant Veri-chips into our hands. In their rush to fight the “Patriot Act”, civil liberties advocates overlooked the insidious spy networks right under their noses.

It is being said by ever-growing crowds, that Facebook is a new breed of spy networks, preparing for the next phase of martial law, by profiling students. A megalomaniac cabal of mass murders who, like all dictatorial regimes, wish to crush all internal dissent and "students" is the first group they'll be paying a visit to. Or at least ones' with an "unacceptable" student past.

You do not need a PhD, or be a rocket scientist to realize that a Tavistock conduit is directly funneled into the Stanford Research Institute, which the new Facebook headquarters is conveniently adjacent to in Menlo Park, California (between Palo Alto and Redwood City). If one is a Facebook user today, your complete chemical, biological, physical, psychological and digital profile has been hardwired into the New World Order's databases. And at any time you should happen to stroke the wrong keys, you will be instantly flagged "an Enemy of the-NWO-State"!

# The Hidden Chapter

William Cooper once warned us about the new-worlders being notorious for having several contingency plans running simultaneously. The grossest misfortune in all of this is that at least one of them might succeed in reaching its final development, not long after you've read this.

We can begin to identify some of the events which appear to have been orchestrated, while pinpointing the ones with the greatest effects upon the masses. This is the only alternative besides lobbying representatives with questions by mail, e-mail, fax, phone and peaceful means of protest. Bill Cooper was killed because he violated the Mason's sacred oath to secrecy by sharing "government secrets". William Cooper once had a very high security clearance with Naval Intelligence, viewing "top secrets" documents every day. Once you cross that line, no matter how serious your findings might be damaging to the public's safety, you immediately become an "Enemy of the State".

(William Cooper 1992 in a CNN interview)

Exploring to bring to the forefront three separate contingency plans I see in motion presently, let's first recall some important statements made in the past by more in the know, than you or I:

- **William Cooper**: "Either there really is a prophecy, such as The Book of Revelations says, or they are using it by creating an assimilation to it...., used as a facade to mislead Christians".

- **Henry Kissinger**: "..., if they were told there was an outright threat from beyond, whether real or promulgated, that threatened our very existence - ..., individual rights will be willingly relinquished for the guarantee of their well-being granted to them by their new world government". (*Reader's note: This is high-treason and conspiracy to overthrow the United States government at the highest degree. Yet black shoplifters go to prison while this man not only gets to roam freely, but is held in high esteem by his Zionist news networks!)

- **Brother Nathanael Kapner** (Former Jew, turned Orthodox Christian): "America will become a Jewish Police State".

- **Israel Shamir**: "Palestine is not the ultimate goal of the Jews; the world is".

(*Reader's note: Sometimes I may refer to New World Order gnomes as either "new-worlders" for NWO, or as "one-worlders for unipolarists.)

O.k. now, it is public knowledge that the U.S. is running an unsustainable deficit while its markets' are now completely rigged and not free-floating, free markets, but are heavily controlled by Wall Street insiders, The Federal Reserve and the U.S. Treasury Department. And it is also public knowledge that the global market is now polluted with between $220 - $260 trillion in toxic derivatives, such as oil-fracking bonds, etc., all intentionally instigated by the same crew. Then we have all the vaults of U.S. gold held at West Point, New York and other locations now being nearly empty. The actual "non-Wharton School of Cooked-book Economics" figures for U.S. unemployment and GDP for the current quarter are roughly 17% to 25% and -1.5 respectively. More than 40% of Americans now receive food from the U.S. government (food stamps). Meanwhile, the Turkish President's family, Israel, the EU and the U.S. are, or had been up until recently:

- Supporting, training, paying, transporting and training ISIS and other terrorists.

- Supporting and promoting with hollow evidence to reason, to hate Muslims, Russia, China and democratically elected, "independent" nations such as Syria.

- Refusing all attempts by Russia and the BRICS nations to become collaborative and peace-seeking.

- Heavily promoting war while inviting a nuclear Armageddon.

If you study all the elements, which are completely manufactured Kool-Aid and orchestration, this economic Ponzi scheme doesn't have much of any life remaining in it. In fact, it is doing all it can to keep the Western economies afloat to the upcoming U.S. presidential elections. So for myself, I can identify 3 possible outcomes to all these events and one of them "will" happen sooner rather than later.

1) A groundswell of widespread, grassroots support will rise up, perhaps sparked by a surprise in the U.S. elections for Bernie Sanders, to successfully turn the tide on several key factors. EU nations will start leaving the NATO and EU memberships and begin to rescue their member nations' economies. This could then be followed by both a decision to completely relinquish NATO and to drop all sanctions imposed against Russia and Iran. This in and of itself would seriously get the global economy's wheels rolling again.

An emergency plan is devised, in coordination with Wall Street to save the Western economies by drawing out the correction into a more slow and gradual correction over time with many very new instruments introduced, like partial amnesty of strategic debts in the system. New versions of Western currencies could then be more feasibly introduced.

2) A more watered-down version of the same scenario, where only several EU nations begin to leave the NATO and EU memberships, as well as remove the sanctions, only it is a more scattered affair and not unanimous, leaving both memberships to sink and relinquish more slowly, in a more sinking Titanic-like fashion.

3) This is "the worst case outcome" with a market crash occuring which will be of historic proportions, much greater than to any extent ever before conceived. This aspect, unless everyone is permitted to soon interrupt NATO and military spending, is evident and irreversible. The destruction of the Western financial system was well thought out in advance and has been compounding that destruction ever since, with an objective to "wring it dry" and not in any way produce a recovery.

The new-worlders have reserved at least three self-created avenues to deflect their blame in any one of these possible outcomes:

a) ISIS and all other terrorists they have created. Or

b) Russia, because the one-worlders have been heavily propagandizing our brains that they're now the West's #1 enemy for no actual, known reason. Or

c) China, which they might blame for its abandoning the U.S. dollar.

So we now have identified three possible contingency outcomes with 3 possible contingent patsies of blame the one-worlders might use. The one-worlders can run their contingencies to also blame this on a World War III, or use it for a reason to start one. But never forget, it will always be due to "anything" but to the true cause which "is them"!

But no one's asking the question here, "What happens the day after"? What will be the likely realities of the collapse of the Western World the day after the markets go through the floor? What will happen immediately is up to 75% of all jobs will cease indefinitely; or operate on a day-to-day basis. Cash too could be worth something at first, but will crash as prices rise. Gold will sky-rocket and all incomes pegged to Social Security and pension-retirement accounts will cease and be made worthless. Banks will seize all cash, or no less than 50%.

Theoretically, the only ones being able to survive will be the holders of precious metals and enough on hand sustainable food products for two years or more (and the Mormons will finally have their day in the Sun). But in the reality sense, these people will be too far outnumbered by the have-nots. Henry Kissinger's dream might then play itself out and the people will "actually ask for Marshall Law" while they beg the new-worlders for food, shelter and safety as the majority of sewer, water and power utilities will go unpaid and be shutting households down like dominoes.

Upon surrendering their remaining rights, all firearms, cash and precious metals will be confiscated, yet redeemed to their "new government". The West's NWO will then portray itself as their savior, issuing them a new currency in the form of "digital credits", a new "food stamps program", "relocation program" (if needed) and "public works job programs", all to safety-net and enable most people to return to a sustainable life, but under very different terms than their former pre-crash ones. Retirees will be given options for reverse mortgages and/or sales by public domain and a large number of them will fall short in meeting most of their needs. Many will be forced to live with families or in government camps.

Millions will die from this completely unnecessary, bleak new Western life and the old adage "America, love it or leave it" will quickly turn into, "Shut-up, you can't leave it"! Much like former East Germany, it will become commonplace for Americans to be machine-gunned down in the back trying to leave. It will be because after all, you will be under the West's New World Order cohorts, who share one-in-the-same affiliation with their past regimes as Hitler-Stalin-Menachem Begin terrorist dictatorships.

As the author I feel my job here is to deliver to you a diverse, rich insight which succeeds in holding your interest and that sparks debate. I can only hope it invokes an activation of the spirit and promotes a peaceful demonstration of grassroots push-back and a participation in democratic ideas, equal collaborations and win-win solutions.

If ever there was a time to "question more" that time has arrived. To foster a passive posturing from this day forward, only removes any last remaining resistance, while making it even easier for the new-worlders to pick you all off, like shooting fish in a barrel.

Author's top 40 selection of suggested authors, columnists, investigative reporters, journalists, news commentators and government officials for further alternative news sources, who can be found online:

Bill Whittle, Brother Nathanael Kapner, Chris Hedges, Cynthia McKinney, Danielle Ryan, Diana Johnstone, Ellen Brown, Eric Zuesse, F. William Engdahl, Gerald Celente, Glenn Greenwald, Gordon Duff, Jamal Kanj, James Corbett, Jim Dean, John Pilger, Jonas Alexis, Julian Assange, Kevin Barrett, Lasha Darkmoon, Maria Zaharova, Marine LePen, Marjorie Cohn, Max Keiser, Michael Krieger, Michael Choudovsky, Mike Adams, Nadi Al-Sakkaf, Nahed Al-Husaini, Nomi Prins, Paul-Craig Roberts, Pepe Escobar, Peter Lavelle, Ralph Nader, Ray McGovern, Sahra Wagenknecht, Stephen Lendman, Tian Wei, Wayne Madsen and Yoichi Shimatsu. (*Reader's note: You may also access all of these from one venue, at the author's blog-site "Cassone' Silk Road News" at: csrn.livejournal.com)

*******

Author’s suggested alternative books:

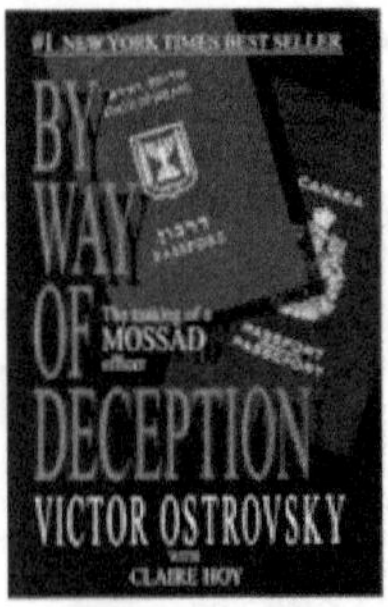


“By Way of Deception” by Victor Ostrovsky

“Trafficking” by Conchita Sarnoff

"Behold a Pale Horse" by William M. Cooper

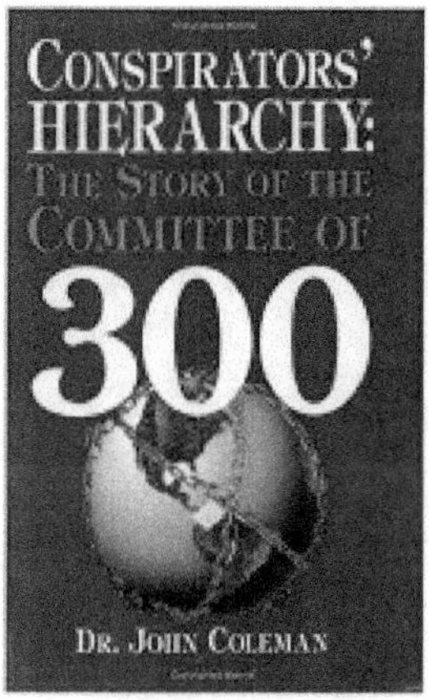


"Conspirator' Hierarchy: The Story of the Committee of 300" by John Coleman

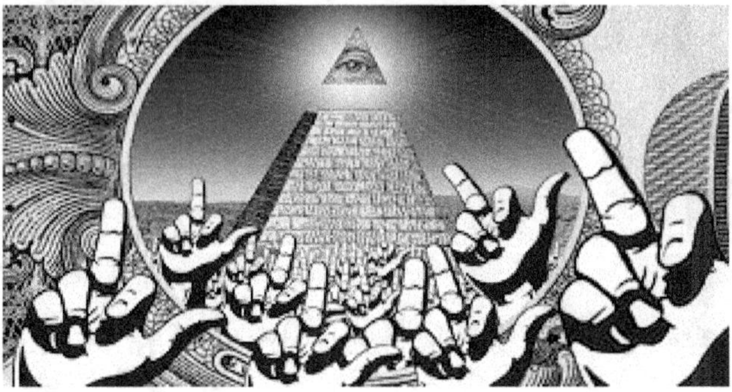

“From Chatham House to Zion, the West’s road to world domination is paved with the souls of affluent, demented men who never knew love, but were stricken with a fever whose lust knew no boundaries and whose hearts knew no contentment”.

Jean-Paul Cassone’

www.ingramcontent.com/pod-product-compliance
Lightning Source LLC
Chambersburg PA
CBHW071337280526
45787CB00001B/129
*9781535009263*